Mapping Educational Success

Revised Edition

SUCCESSFUL SCHOOLS
Guidebooks to Effective Educational Leadership
Fenwick W. English, Series Editor

Mapping Educational Success

Strategic Thinking and Planning for School Administrators

Revised Edition

Roger Kaufman

CORWIN PRESS, INC.
A Sage Publications Company
Thousand Oaks, California

For information address:

 Corwin Press, Inc.
A Sage Publications Company
2455 Teller Road
Thousand Oaks, California 91320

SAGE Publications Ltd.
6 Bonhill Street
London EC2A 4PU
United Kingdom

SAGE Publications India Pvt. Ltd.
M-32 Market
Greater Kailash I
New Delhi 110 048 India

Printed in the United States of America

Library of Congress Cataloging-in-Publication Data

Kaufman, Roger A.
   Mapping educational success : strategic thinking and planning for school administrators / Roger Kaufman. — Rev. ed.
      p.   cm. – (Successful schools ; 1)
   Includes bibliographical references (pp. 176-181) and index.
   ISBN 0-8039-6203-7
   1. Educational planning–United States. 2. Strategic planning–United States. 3. School management and organization–United States. I. Title. II. Series.
   LC89.K38   1995
   371.2'07–dc20   94-22986

95 96 97 98 99 10 9 8 7 6 5 4 3 2 1
Corwin Press Production Editor: Marie Louise Penchoen

Contents

Foreword

Planners and planning systems and models come and go, but Roger Kaufman has been one of the pillars of the planning community for more than three decades. He has written best-selling books that have been translated into many languages and has long been known for his work in schools and educational systems.

Planning is essentially, and most important, a *conceptual* business as opposed to an *activity*. Most practitioners get all bogged down in the "activity." They see planning as the "doing" as opposed to the "thinking." What Kaufman's approach has always done is to reverse this emphasis. You place your emphasis first on *how to think about planning* because how one thinks about it fundamentally shapes what one "does" in the activity as well as the *utility* of what emanates from the process once it is completed. This, by the way, is what the Kaufman approach is all about. It is not some new "technology" or gadget or fandango. It isn't a "thing." What makes it different or *hard* for many people is that Kaufman really requires them to think differently on the conceptual level. So administrators don't initially *do anything*. Rather, they have to learn to "see" and "conceptualize" in a different way than typical school culture and tradition may dictate.

I'm convinced that many problems don't get solved in education because people are trained to avoid them by simply adopting a conceptual framework that eliminates "seeing" them altogether. The most successful people in this "solution culture" are problem avoiders, not problem solvers. The roots of really solving problems tie right back into how one conceptualizes what a problem is. In this cycle, "we" are part of the problem and paradoxically its solution. The successful planning that Roger Kaufman has taught me over many years is to tie *the planner* into that cycle.

In this respect, the Kaufman approach is different because it moves the planner as a kind of inert, so-called objective party looking at "them and their problems" into a more realistic and subjective state where the planner's outlook is intimately part of the problem and its resolution. Kaufman dissolves the "objective-subjective" distinction in this very small but critical maneuver.

School administrators have to learn to put themselves *into* the planning process because their outlook, values, biases, and life experiences become the basis for their inclusion in the conceptualization of what planning is. They can't stand apart from this process and "guide it." They have to realize that their inclusion in it is the only way out of the box. This forces them to examine their own biases and to reconnect their own work to real outcomes instead of the false promises of fads and new gimmicks.

Upon reflection, I believe that what makes the Kaufman approach better, but harder, is that it isn't flashy like some of the more popular but shallow models that don't require much different thinking on the part of the participants. Rather, it forces the *planner* to change the actual *thinking about* planning before he or she "does" anything.

I am reminded of the quotation by Sir Joshua Reynolds that Edison used to post in his lab, which read: "There is no expedient to which a man will not resort to avoid the real labor of thinking." Edison used to declare, "My business is thinking." The Kaufman planning model is primarily about thinking more than anything else. It is also why many practitioners (and many planners I might add) will resist the approach because it initially strikes them as too "ivory tower." But nothing could be further from the truth.

This small volume stands as a concise and practical application by one of the grand masters of educational planning. We are proud to have it in our series.

FENWICK W. ENGLISH
University of Kentucky

Preface

This revised book is for principals and administrators who want to make a difference—not by trying to work harder and longer but by fashioning a new educational reality that builds on what currently works and adding what is missing. It is for practical humanists who care enough about learners, teachers, parents, and communities to make a difference, with no blaming, no name calling, no excuses.

Education's problems cannot be attributed to any one source. Just about everyone is doing what they presume is right, and our results are not getting much better. Let's not complain, let's build. This book describes what to do in getting the kind of educational success and payoffs we all want; it is about being strategic: how to think and perform smarter. Being strategic and acting strategically are the essential ingredients in planning and delivering successful education.

I wrote this book and this revision based upon my years of experience with both public and private sector organizations. I bear witness to the fact that positive and efficient change can happen. All it takes is commitment to results, the learners, success, and continuous improvement.

This commitment often requires moving outside of our usual comfort zones and taking the sensible risk of shifting from a means and resources orientation to one where results are always in central focus. This strategic shift leads to different methods of planning, developing, implementing, evaluating, and renewing—while leading to predictable success.

The basics of being strategic are straightforward. This book provides the "whats," "whys," and "hows" of strategic thinking and includes six *Critical Success Factors* useful in defining and achieving success, basic educational questions to be asked and answered, and optional areas of emphasis for principals (whose primary concern is for their school and learner performance) and for administrators (whose primary concern is the entire educational system and its societal payoffs and contributions).

In addition, there are guides and aids to help you and other educators define and achieve strategic success. There is also a Troubleshooting Guide, which poses frequently experienced problems and redirects you to discussions on how to deal with them.

Being strategic is more than planning, more than operations, more than humanism, and more than management, although these are all essential ingredients. Strategic thinking is how you act day to day in defining what kind of world you want for tomorrow's child; what your system and all of its schools, classes, and resources can contribute to that future; and relating what you do and how you do it to a shared vision of tomorrow.

Here is a brief outline of this revised book. It is written and designed to help you and your educational partners be strategic.

Strategic Thinking: What and Why

Chapter 1 deals with overcoming single-issue thinking and becoming proactive—not just reacting to crises and pressures. Basic concepts and tools for being strategic are provided, including being ready to get out of your comfort zone, separating ends and means, defining who is to be the primary client and beneficiary of the educational system, relating the three levels of educational planning and results, and identifying why schools fail (and what to do about it).

A Framework and Basic Concepts for Strategic Thinking and Planning

Being strategic requires a practical framework, a correct and shared destination, and appropriate tools. Chapter 2 provides a three-phase framework, and basic tools and concepts, including setting directions; the relationships among three levels of results; and how to relate educational resources, efforts, results, and consequences.

Objectives and Needs Assessment: Basic Building Blocks

Being strategic builds upon essential tools, including measurable objectives and needs assessment (which is often talked about but seldom defined and used rationally). Chapter 3 shows how to prepare useful objectives, from mission objectives to detailed learner performance specifications; how to define and develop needs and needs assessments as well as quasi needs and quasi needs assessments; "hard" (independently verifiable) and "soft" (personal and subjective) data; and seven basic questions that any educational organization should ask and answer.

Mega-Level Planning: The Larger Community and Society

Mega-level thinking and planning are the administrator's choice when the primary client and beneficiary are an educational organization's community and society—the topic of Chapter 4. Included are how to define and use an ideal vision and the tools, techniques, and steps of mega-level needs assessment.

Macro-Level Planning: The District or School

Macro-level thinking and planning are of special concern to principals and central office administrators when the primary client and beneficiary is the educational organization itself. The tools, techniques, and steps of macro planning and needs assessment are provided in Chapter 5.

Micro-Level Planning: People, Programs, Courses

When the primary beneficiary is an educational organization's internal clients—teachers, learners, courses, activities—use the micro level. This level is of special interest to principals. Strategic and tactical planning are often confused, and Chapter 6 differentiates between them and shows their relationship. The tools, techniques, and steps of micro-level planning are provided.

Completing the Plan and Putting It to Work

Chapter 7 details how to develop the Strategic Action Plan, including operational planning, methods-means analysis, quasi needs assessments (often confused with real needs assessments), systems analysis methods (which provide the criteria for selecting the methods and means), how to complete the strategic plan, (including appropriate report elements), continuous improvement through "Total Quality Management", and a rational extension of conventional approaches called "Quality Management Plus."

Strategic Thinking in Action

Chapter 8 details how you can keep problems from arising in the first place as well as what to do when troubles do arise, with the ultimate educational troubleshooting kit.

A Hypothetical Case

Chapter 9 contains a case study: "A Hypothetical Case: Strategic Thinking in Sleightown School District."

Acknowledgments

In reality, no one author writes a book. This revised volume reflects many, many contributions that directly and indirectly helped shape the useful parts of this work. (I alone am responsible for that which fails to meet quality standards.) Let me recognize the most visible contributors:

At the Center for Needs Assessment and Planning at Florida State University: Kathi Watters edited, argued, suggested, and contributed to the coherence; Phil Grisé (the Associate Director) made suggestions on the contents; Leon Sims constantly reminded me of reality and application in the operational world of education; Jason Strickland turned my scribbles into the figures and tables; and Jean Van Dyke did final manuscript preparation.

Educational Technology Magazine, Training & Development Journal, and *Performance & Instruction Journal,* all in the spirit of professional sharing, allowed me to use (usually in modified form) material from some of my articles.

Sage Publications also allowed me to use (again, usually in modified form) excerpts from my books published by them. As part of acknowledging Sage, it should be understood that this book does not replace other referenced works: *Strategic Planning in Education: Rethinking, Restructuring, Revitalizing* (Kaufman & Herman); *Planning Educational Systems* (Kaufman); and *Strategic Planning Plus: An Organizational Guide* (Kaufman), which supply details, rationale, and methods for delivering on what this book suggests.

I would also like to acknowledge the graduate students at Florida State University; the consulting clients and participants in workshops and seminars throughout the world; and colleagues everywhere who care enough about education and me to force critical thinking; Fen English, who invited this book and gave me important suggestions; and Gracia Alkema, who is publishing it; as well as the professionals who read this and apply it make a better world for our children and grandchildren.

ROGER KAUFMAN
Florida State University

About the Author

Roger Kaufman is Professor of Educational Research, and Director of the Center for Needs Assessment and Planning, at Florida State University. He is also affiliated with the faculty of industrial engineering and management systems at the University of Central Florida. He has served as Professor at the U.S. International University and at Chapman University, both in California. He earned his Ph.D. (Communications) from New York University, an M.A. (psychology and industrial engineering) from Johns Hopkins, and a B.A. (psychology, sociology, and statistics) from George Washington University.

In addition, he has held positions in the private sector, including Boeing, the Martin Company, US Industries, and Douglas Aircraft. His consulting clients include educational systems, governments, and corporations in the United States, Canada, Latin America, Europe, New Zealand, and Australia. He is a Fellow in Educational Psychology of the American Psychological Association and a Diplomate in School Psychology of the American Board of Professional Psychology. He has been named "Member for Life"—their highest honor—by the National Society for Performance and Instruction, an organization in which he served as president. He was the 1983 Haydn Williams Fellow at the Curtin University of Technology in Perth, Australia. He has published 28 books on strategic planning, needs assessment, management, and evaluation and is the author of more than 150 articles on those topics.

1

Strategic Thinking: What and Why

1.1 Education: What's Our Role and How Are We Doing?

We are probably doing as good a job of education as can be done if we don't challenge many basic assumptions about schools, schooling, and the delivery of instruction. We have hit our "upper limit," where spending more time and money in trying to do better what we already do well will be disappointing (Branson, 1987, 1991; Perelman, 1989, 1990). U.S. education is apparently the most labor-intensive activity in the world: 93% of the U.S. budget goes to labor costs as compared with 54% in the average business. As of 1990, the United States spent proportionately less of its gross national product on education than most other nations (Rasell & Mishel, 1990) but was spending more than all but Switzerland on per-pupil instructional outlays (Perelman, 1990).

Teachers—good professionals—labor long and hard during their more than nine months in the classroom. They work with a lot of students, often in overcrowded rooms. The cultural diversity and various value systems the learners bring with them provide a challenge unseen in other nations. Armed only with the conventional ways of thinking about funding and delivering education, today's teachers are doing as well as (if not better than) can be expected. They are doing it, largely, by incorporating methods and materials used on them in their youth. The knowledge base has changed, learner characteristics have changed, and society has changed. But education still attempts to do better by working harder and spending more instead of by defining what its business is.[1]

For their part, principals, administrators, and board members really want good things to happen for students. Educators receive often conflicting and predominately single-issue marching orders from federal and state legislators and are under constant threat from pressure groups (and their lawyers) to react with one quick fix after another. Board members, as part of the educational team, get conflicting messages from their constituents concerning what education should do and deliver. Everyone seems to know how education should be done, and people are not bashful about letting others know.

Albert Einstein observed that our world is characterized by a proliferation of means and a confusion of goals (cited in Kaufman, 1972). We argue about how education should do its job, but we do not have clear purposes toward which to steer. We are working as hard now as we know how to work. But that won't improve education's contribution to learners and our shared world.

A. *Working Harder Won't Make Us More Successful*

It is widely recognized that U.S. education is in trouble and has been for many years. The source of the trouble attracts wide debate, however (see, for example, Banathy, 1991; Branson, 1987; Cuban, 1990; Kirst & Meister, 1985; Newmann, 1991; Perelman, 1990; Pipho, 1991; Rasell & Mishel, 1990). Suggestions for "true reform" vary anywhere from tinkering with the hours of school and teacher's pay to changing our form of government!

The trouble *is not* bad or deceitful people, selfish unions, uncaring teachers, stupid administrators, quick-fix boards of education, unfeeling legislators, or political revolutionaries. The troubles are more than racism, sexism, or exploitation, although these elements make the situation deteriorate even more. Recognizing our maladies, legislators have piled laws upon educators, each one intending to fix the situation once and for all. Legislation, regardless of how well meaning, has seemed only to raise hopes without delivering useful consequences. Legislated and conventional approaches to "fixing" education seem to ebb and flow like the tides that rush in only to recede and be replaced by another wave, shifting from teacher-centered to learner-centered instruction, curriculum reforms focused on student-choice to a common core, and centralized administration to local control (Cuban, 1990).[2] As the initiatives fail (Kirst & Meister, 1985), the legislatures react and attempt to solve educational performance problems by laws and not by strategic thinking. We care, but change alone—without clear and useful purpose—will result in frustration and failure.

Simply changing the labels for what we do ("restructuring," "reengineering," "benchmarking," "outcome-based education," and the like) will not work. We must change the way we *think* about education and shift from budget-driven strategies to strategy-driven budgets. The rhetoric in education has too long concerned results, while the practice has usually regressed into placing new labels on process- and resource-related activities. Performance—useful performance—has to take center stage. The demand for clear purpose—education mission objectives—is clear and beyond doubt (Pipho, 1991). Yet many reform/restructuring/change initiatives assume that the objectives for education are known, clear, and shared. Not so: We keep turning to changes in how we do education without first defining where we are going, and why we want to get there, and obtaining a shared commitment for both the journey and the destination.

B. *Caring*

We care about our learners. We spend money on them, talk about their well-being, and turn to legislators for help. We recognize that a competent individual is the core and soul of both a caring society and a competitive work force. We have tried many approaches—local, state, and national—to improve the payoffs of our education labors and dollars. The approaches regularly seem to fall short of their promise. And we still care.

Caring alone is not enough. Passing new and ambitious laws alone is not enough. Neither are spending more money or tinkering with the processes of teaching enough. We must stop selecting single-variable/single-issue responses to address our concerns. We must *change*: revitalize our schools and our resolve, rethink our goals and purposes, and restructure our educational system so that it works smarter—more effectively and efficiently (Banathy, 1991; Kaufman, Herman, & Watters, in press). We must shift from a preoccupation with resources and methods to a primary concern for creating the kind of world in which we want tomorrow's child to live.

C. *Change*

Change has been used so often that its mere mention brings inner distrust. Educators have been asked to change over the years—from one splintered, single quick fix or one superficial idea to another. We mistrust appeals to change because we often know that what is offered is either counterfeit or cosmetic. One catalyst prompting change comes from a misguided notion that educators and parents are basically naive (and/or lazy) and cannot understand complex issues and concepts. Another source of change stems from a lack of understanding of educational size and scope. So, simplistic and fragmented responses are attempted. Still another source of change flows from the failure to link educational resources and processes to in-school and societal results and payoffs. Consequently, we talk about process and hope useful results will follow. This book, however, is not talking about superficial change (which should be restrained) but about fundamental shifts: justifiable, useful, and caring change.

D. *Shifting How We View and Interact With Our World*

We tend to teach subjects and not learners. We accept without question that the sum total of conventional courses (math, science, music, and so on) will provide all learners with what they have to know and be able to do for current and future survival, self-sufficiency, and well-being. Figure 1.1 shows the conventional subject-based planning tactics. But what about the "blank spaces"[3] (total requirements for future functioning) not covered by conventional content areas? How will learners master what is not available in the curriculum?

We splinter our curriculum and content and thus miss both the coverage of vital areas as well as the synergies among topics and areas. If we start educational (and curriculum) planning with a big picture—what learners have to know and be able to do in tomorrow's world—the educational experiences will be more complete, responsive, and useful.

E. *The Rediscovery of System Thinking*

We are rediscovering system approach concepts (see Senge, 1990). Instead of splitting, dissecting, and dissociating parts of a system (concentrating on courses, not on the entire educational/social system; tinkering with teaching and methods instead of defining the ideal vision and objectives), the holistic view of organizations as subsystems of a larger world is becoming reaffirmed (see, for example, Banathy, 1987, 1991; Banghart, 1969; Bertalanffy, 1968; Churchman, 1969/1975; Cleland & King, 1968; Corrigan & Corrigan, 1985; Corrigan & Kaufman, 1966; Gagne, 1962; Kaufman, 1968, 1972, 1988b, 1992b; Morgan & Chadwick, 1971). A system approach views education as the sum of the

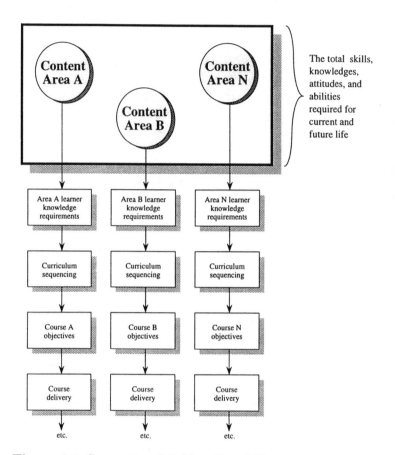

Figure 1.1. Conventional Subject-Based Planning Tactics
NOTE: By splintering curriculum and learning sequences into disciplines, or content areas, we don't include the "blank spaces" of what education should deliver.

independent parts working together and individually to achieve a common purpose. A change in any part changes all others.

A basic secret (really a rational technique) for defining and achieving success is also to find the correct destination for the system before tinkering with the internal parts and resources. To set a useful direction, we have to be open both to considering changes in what we now do and also to rethinking where we should be heading.[4]

1.2 Changing the Way We View the World: Shifting Paradigms and Mental Gears

A. *Realities of the World: People, Values, and Demands Don't Stand Still*

We require a major shift in how we think and transact with our world. Peter Senge (1990) suggests the term *metanoia* be resurrected as the appropriate label for a shift of mind. This book is about the whys, whats, and hows of such a mind shift in education. Thomas Kuhn (1962) told us about paradigm shifts: moving from one set of assumed boundaries and operating rules to another. Joel Arthur Barker describes this phenomenon clearly and convincingly in his videotapes *The Business of Paradigm* and *Paradigm Pioneers* in his Discovering the Future Series.[5] The evidence of opportunities lost because we used old assumptions and refused to accept that there was a paradigm shift are all around us: The Swiss, rejecting digital watches (their own invention), lost most of the world market; the United States, disbelieving it was important to improve auto design and fuel efficiency, gave overseas manufacturers a huge chunk of our automotive business.

As the world changes and we persist in applying old boundaries and outmoded rules to new realities, we fall behind and increasingly have to run to keep up until we drop of exhaustion. In education, we may be experiencing the same kind of drain, in spite of our very best efforts and continued investments. Where once we focused on means and resources to deliver useful results, it is now time that we realize these older ways don't deal with new realities, new parameters. The new educational paradigm is one of contributing to societally useful results, not simply teaching subjects to kids and hoping for the best.

We can stop being self-limiting and open ourselves to new directions and opportunities based on new realities. Because most conventional approaches don't deliver the results we must have, it is riskier to continue what we are now doing than it is to shift to new boundaries—parameters—and new rules for thinking, planning, and doing. So important is being open and enterprising that it is the first—and overarching—"Critical Success Factor."

> *Critical Success Factor 1*: Move out of today's comfort zones and use new and wider boundaries for thinking, planning, doing, and evaluating.

B. *Do We Really Have to Change Our Ways?*

Do we really have to move from our current paradigms— understandings and assumptions—of how education works? If we aren't the masters of change, we will be the victims of it. If we only curse today's problems and solutions, we will not be open to creating a new education and a new reality. Critical Success Factor 1 is important for being strategic. Without it, we will likely prove Drucker right when he reminds us that we are getting better and better at doing that which should not be done at all.

C. *Politics: "They" Will Never Let It Happen*

Another self-defeating factor in strategic thinking is the conventional assumption that the political and economic forces— "they"—won't allow positive change to happen. The argument is that the powers that be are simply retaining the stranglehold on cheap labor to exploit citizens by preparing them solely for desperate lives in the sweatshops of big business. Unfortunately, while pockets of despots still exist, the emerging reality is that the ways of exploiting people as replaceable parts in the dehumanizing maw of industry are just not feasible any more. Business has changed, so has education, although neither has yet targeted the widest-angle missions. But that, too, is coming.

In fact, the stubborn attitude that people are not important, and are as interchangeable as machine parts, is as outdated as the dinosaur.[6] Acknowledged futurists (e.g., Naisbitt & Aburdene,

1990; Toffler, 1990) and management gurus (Kanter, 1989; Peters, 1987; Rummler & Brache, 1990) recognize that everyone in an organization is important and that knowledge, ability, and technical skills will differentiate the successful organizations from those that fail. Toffler (1990) suggests that the new chasms in society will not be between the rich and poor or the Left and Right but between the information rich and the information poor. Educated, contributing, competent, and caring people—human capital—are back on central stage in our new era.

D. *Choosing to Be Successful, Not Just Comfortable*

The way we view our world is up to us. Is it a view where simply working harder will get us demanded results, or is it one where we must work smarter? It is our choice to open ourselves to responsible and responsive change—in spite of the way we always have done it—and move out of our comfort zone when reality rears its head. And one of the first things to jostle our comfort zone is direction setting: Where are we now headed in education, and where should we be going?

1.3 Strategic Thinking: Setting Our Direction

Educational success—providing learners with the skills, knowledge, attitudes, and abilities to be self-sufficient, self-reliant, competent, caring, and mutually interdependent adults—is more than writing measurable objectives for courses. It encompasses more than preparing new and tougher graduation or vocational standards. Strategic thinking depends upon developing an *ideal vision* of tomorrow and identifying the contributions our schools, curriculum, and methods will make to reaching that *preferred future* (Kaufman & Herman, 1991a, 1991b). The process for getting from our current caring to our future success is simple, practical, and straightforward. It is as simple as changing from a means orientation to an ends focus. It is as practical as making certain that all educational partners have a common guiding star toward which all can steer while making their unique contributions. It is as straightforward as knowing that we should be concerned with our future simply because we will be spending the rest of our lives there. As Mager (1975) so deftly points out, if we don't know where we are going, we could end up someplace else.

A. Reacting to Economic and Social Realities

The triumph of conventional wisdom in education. The world is changing, and education and educators *react*. The media tell us Americans are losing the productivity and economic battle to Japan and Germany. The gap in productivity between the United States and other advancing nations is closing, but we are not "dead" yet (Naisbitt & Aburdene, 1990; Toffler, 1990). We react to an impending crisis by adopting Total Quality Management initiatives. It is the age of technology, and schools now have computers that are often used for recreation. We have an increasingly diverse learner population, so we hire teachers on the basis of their ethnicity, not also for their competence.[7]

B. We Care, but We Don't Really Know What to Deliver and Do

Success can come from thinking strategically, not from simply throwing more money and people at the schools. We can work much smarter than we are. Although it might be satisfying to conduct political and/or economic postmortems on failed and enduring school reforms (see, for example, Carnoy & Levin, 1976; Kirst & Meister, 1985), the strong possibility remains that educational planning is done backward—we react to social pressures rather than being proactive, defining the kind of world we want tomorrow's child to live in and then identifying what contribution education and schools can and should make.

Caring is not enough. Changing is not enough. Spending more money is not enough. Raising standards is not enough. In fact, each of the single-issue, quick fixes imposed upon education might be failing for the wrong reasons.

C. *Time to Work Smarter*

It is imperative to look at education from a different perspective. Taking a different view usually requires us to suspend judgment temporarily on our current understandings, beliefs, values, and ways that we relied on up to now—being ready to shift out of one's own comfort zone. Ready?

We have been selecting means (hows) before agreeing upon the ends. It is now time to get ends and means related. Being strategic is knowing what to achieve, being able to justify the direction, and then finding the best ways to get there.

D. *Ends and Means*

If there is *one most important element*—after being open to change—to successful strategic thinking, it is to know the difference between ends and means. Perhaps no other area is more confused and more simple to resolve.

Ends are results, consequences, accomplishments, and pay-offs delivered. There are several different levels of ends, but they deal with results. Ends include citizens who are self-sufficient and self-reliant; graduates, completers, people earning a license in a trade; students having acquired a specific skill, passed a test or course, completed a recital.

Means are the ways to deliver ends. For strategic thinking and planning, means include the resources (time, money, people, facilities) and methods (teaching, learning, supervising, planning, thinking, developing).

Differentiating between ends and means is the most vital action you can take. Yet it is the one shift that people find most difficult. Perhaps it's like knowing that a healthy diet will allow you to live longer but being unwilling to give up the old habits.

> *Critical Success Factor 2*: Differentiate between ends and means (distinguish between what and how).

If you start looking at the world, including education, as the relationships—including differences—between ends and means, you will focus on what is to be accomplished before deciding how to progress. By distinguishing between ends and means, the differences between mastery and competence (results, or ends) versus teaching and learning (how-to's, or means) becomes clear.

Some education-related ends and means appear in Table 1.1. Cover the two right-hand columns with a sheet of paper and sort each of the items into their appropriate classification, either ends or means. Then compare your choices with those in the right-hand columns of the table.

We spend most of our time and money on means, but starting with means before defining useful ends is backward. It is vital to identify first what results (ends) we should accomplish. Looking back upon the myriad educational reforms, note that almost all of them (team teaching, differentiated staffing, decentralization, national testing, computer-assisted learning, Total Quality Management) are means to loosely defined ends. In fact, most of our *professed* educational ends are means. To prove this, retrieve your district's education mission. Sort the various elements into means and ends and note how much attention is given to means.

Figure 1.2 provides an algorithm—a job aid that contains yes/no questions and related functions—for determining whether your objectives are ends related and whether they relate to what learners must accomplish in school and beyond.

1.4 Who Is the Primary Client of What Gets Planned and Delivered?

Differences in educational planning approaches are dependent upon who is identified as the primary client and beneficiary of the "deliverables." Three major client choices are available:

1. citizens, taxpayers, residents, and members of the society and community;
2. the school or school system itself; and

TABLE 1.1 Some Typical Educational Ends and Means

	END	MEANS
Restructuring		X
School-Based Managing		X
Competency-Based Test Item	X	
Total Quality Management		X
Teaching		X
Learning		X
Course Grade	X	
Graduation	X	
Employment	X	
Budget		X
Planning		X
Computer-Assisted Instructing		X
Open Enrollments		X
Decentralization		X
Unionization		X
Law		X
Policy		X
Curriculum		X
Classrooms		X
Child Care Program		X
School Lunch Program		X

3. individuals or small groups—internal clients (such as teachers, learners, subject matter areas)—within the school or system.

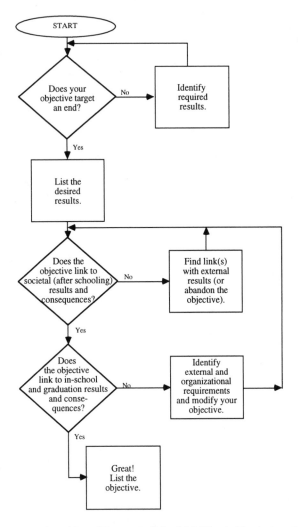

Figure 1.2. An Algorithm: A Job Aid That Contains Yes/No Questions and Related Functions
NOTE: Use these questions to determine whether your objectives are ends related and whether they relate to what learners must accomplish in school and beyond.

When the primary client and beneficiary is the society and community, then planning is at the *mega* level. When the clients are the school or educational system itself, planning is at the *macro* level. When the beneficiaries are individuals and small groups, then we are planning at the *micro* level.

Who are we planning for? If education is the solution, what's the problem?

A. *Asking and Answering the "Right" Questions*

Strategic thinking, and consequent planning and accomplishments, depend upon useful direction finding:

1. Where should our educational system be headed?
2. Why do we want to get there?

Seven questions that any educational organization should ask and answer appear in Table 1.2. Any organization is a means to societal ends. As such, each should be concerned with identifying the societal payoffs it delivers. There are *seven questions education organizations may consider* as well as the primary level of concern for each shown in Table 1.2; they will be referred to throughout this book.

Although these seven questions might seem simplistic to some—"everyone will say 'yes' to them"—the reality is that there are some who (a) want to leave Question 1 to those in power and/or (b) are only interested in Questions 5, 6, and 7. Of course, all seven questions exist, regardless of whether we formally address them.

Caring plus commitment. Another related question follows on the heals of a "yes" answer to the seven questions. For each, the follow-on question is this: "Do you care about this enough to commit to its accomplishment?" Thus everyone who is an educational partner should both care about as well as commit to getting all of the required results.

B. *The Three Levels of Educational Results*

Often overlooked in educational thinking, planning, and evaluation is the fact that there are three levels of results. The most basic (Question 1) has a *mega* focus because it is concerned with

TABLE 1.2 Asking the Right Questions: Seven Basic Questions All Educators Should Ask (and answer)

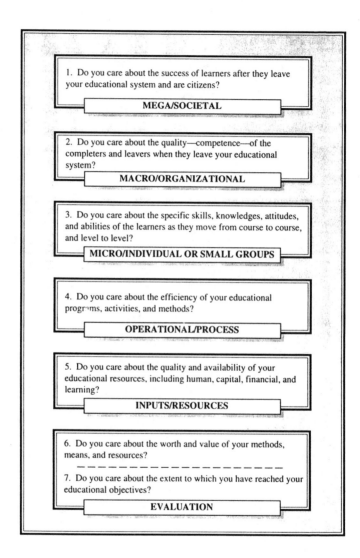

1. Do you care about the success of learners after they leave your educational system and are citizens?

MEGA/SOCIETAL

2. Do you care about the quality—competence—of the completers and leavers when they leave your educational system?

MACRO/ORGANIZATIONAL

3. Do you care about the specific skills, knowledges, attitudes, and abilities of the learners as they move from course to course, and level to level?

MICRO/INDIVIDUAL OR SMALL GROUPS

4. Do you care about the efficiency of your educational programs, activities, and methods?

OPERATIONAL/PROCESS

5. Do you care about the quality and availability of your educational resources, including human, capital, financial, and learning?

INPUTS/RESOURCES

6. Do you care about the worth and value of your methods, means, and resources?

————————————————

7. Do you care about the extent to which you have reached your educational objectives?

EVALUATION

societal and community outcomes and consequences. The most usual focus of educational missions is at the *macro* level: the agency or school level (Question 2), which is concerned with the contributions, or outputs, of the organization itself. Still a third level is the *micro:* being concerned with individual products or small group accomplishments (Question 3), such as a course completed or a test passed.

These three levels of results are "nested": Mega results are built up from macro-level ones, which in turn are an integration and collection of micro-level results. The three levels of results form the third Critical Success Factor:

> *Critical Success Factor 3*: Use all three levels of results (mega, macro, and micro).

Although we educators spend most of our time and effort in doing things—delivering learning opportunities—our thinking and planning often starts at the how-to and the resources level. We rush into action before confirming direction. Activities and resources are important and must be sensibly linked to our objectives. Thus Questions 4 and 5 are concerned with the operations of any educational agency.

Questions 1, 2, and 3 address educational results. Questions 4 and 5 deal with methods and resources.

By correctly linking the three levels of results and relating means to ends, we may strategically design and deliver useful education. To do less would risk doing what Peter Drucker warns against: getting better and better at doing that which should not be done at all. Figure 1.3 provides an algorithm that will better assure our being strategic.

Note that strategic thinking does not assume that the only way to help learners is through courses or even education. Other agencies (health, labor, charities, and so on) might better meet learner needs alone or in cooperation with education.

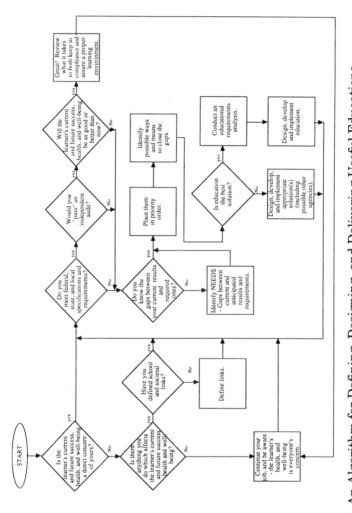

Figure 1.3. An Algorithm for Defining, Designing, and Delivering Useful Educations

NOTE: In this algorithm, the learner's current and future success, health, and well-being are the primary concern of all educators.

TABLE 1.3 Relating Four Educational "Reforms" to Critical Success Factors 2 and 3

	CRITICAL SUCCESS FACTORS			
	#2		#3	
	Yes	No	Yes	No
Restructuring		X		X
School-Based Management		X		X
Competency-Based Test Item	X			X
Total Quality Management		X		X

1.5 Why Our Educational Problems Persist

Earlier, we noted how educational problems persist and how the same solutions seem to reappear at regular intervals. This is not amazing once we realize that, in the past and in spite of good intentions, we have *failed* to

(a) link educational purposes to the mega level;
(b) plan on the basis of ends, not means;
(c) integrate all three levels of results (mega ↔ macro ↔ micro); and
(d) accept old ground rules and boundaries as changed to a new paradigm: from a means to an ends orientation.

Stated differently, our past behavior has ignored Critical Success Factors 2 and 3 (and thus probably 1). Let's revisit some of the means and ends identified earlier. We have already noted that many reforms, such as restructuring, Total Quality Management, and school-based management, were means, not ends. Identify the extent to which Critical Success Factors 2 and 3 have been considered in selecting these reforms, as shown in Table 1.3.

Although many well-intentioned educational reforms hope for good results, they are usually selected with nothing more than the fervent hope that useful results will follow. The lives of learners and our future citizens are far more important than to tie educational thinking, planning, restructuring, reforms, and evaluation only to hope. Applying Critical Success Factors 1, 2, and 3 will reduce that risk.

A. *Proactive and Reactive Thinking and Planning*

When creating new directions and purposes, our thinking is proactive. Waiting until we must respond to situations, our thinking becomes reactive. Questions 1 through 5 (in Table 1.2) are proactive concerns: strategic thinking and planning. Reactive concerns are addressed by Questions 6 and 7; evaluation is after the fact.

B. *Which of the Seven Questions Can We Afford to Eliminate?*

Which questions can we afford to omit? Which ones do we not currently formally account for in our thinking, planning, and doing? Ask yourself and your educational partners which of the seven questions can be avoided or which are not the concern of everyone? I hope that all agree: All seven questions are vital.

Teachers, principals, administrators, board members, and citizens will have different levels of emphasis, but they all care about the seven questions. Table 1.4 identifies primary and secondary concerns for major educational partners. Because one group has the primary concern and responsibility for a question does not negate its importance to others. Every educational partner should be concerned with all questions and ensure his or her contribution to each one. In the complex organizational world, everyone cannot look after all aspects of education. We must agree on the array of questions we will ask and answer, then rely on others to do their jobs competently. Notice that everyone has a primary concern with Question 7—results.

TABLE 1.4 Primary and Secondary Concerns for Major Educational Partners

	QUESTION NUMBER (FROM TABLE 1.2)						
PARTNER	1	2	3	4	5	6	7
Principals	S	P	P	P	P	P	P
Teachers	S	S	P	P	P	P	P
Administrator	P	P	P	S	S	S	P
Board	P	P	S	S	S	S	P
Community	P	P	S	S	S	S	P

NOTE: While all educational partners are concerned with all seven questions, they have different primary emphases. Note that there are no questions that are not addressed both primarily and secondarily by one or more of the partners. Key: P = primary concern and responsibility; S = secondary concern.

Teachers will find most of their strategic issues covered in Chapter 6, "Micro-Level Planning: People, Programs, Courses." Central office administrators and board members will find their responsibilities detailed in Chapter 5, "Macro-Level Planning: The District or School," and in Chapter 4, "Mega-Level Planning: The Larger Community and Society."

c. Change, Apprehension, Hostility, and One's Comfort Zone

Everyone, as noted earlier, has a territory, or zone, in which he or she operates comfortably: no hassles, no problems, no surprises. Our day-to-day tranquility depends upon operating where we know the ground rules and where our behavior and that of others is predictable and under control. We come to expect our

TABLE 1.5 The Degree of Relative Comfort/Discomfort with the Basic Education Questions (from Table 1.2)

Basic Education Question # (from Table 1.2)	Usual Zone of Comfort/Discomfort			
	Very Comfortable	Comfortable	Uneasy	Frequent Discomfort
1				X
2			X	
3		X		
4, 5, 6	X			
7-Micro		X	?	
7-Macro			X	?
7-Mega				X

NOTE: The ? for Question 7 indicates that some, but not all, people get uneasy with evaluation at that level.

homes to be islands of tranquility in an otherwise chaotic world, and we would like our workplaces to be the same.

Then, along comes change. The change might be a new accountability law, the resignation of someone competent, a new organizational chart, or a new school board member. Most change really looks more ominous than it turns out to be, but other change can start pushing us to the edge of, and even beyond, our comfort zone.

Using mega-level planning often jostles people's comfort zone boundaries and, before calm consideration is given, apprehension and sometimes hostility take over. The most troublesome challenge comes from Question 1, which asks if we care (enough to do something) about how well learners do after they leave our system and become citizens. Table 1.5 shows relative comfort zone areas and the questions (from Table 1.2) that fall within each.

While becoming strategic, be aware that some people might react as the ideas and concepts challenge traditional comfort zone boundaries. Not all change is useful, and not all assaults on our tranquility are valid, but mega planning and the seven questions (in Table 1.2) are worthy of serious and calm consideration, even if they push you beyond the point of tranquility. The willingness to go outside one's own paradigm and ground rules to create a better tomorrow is the first Critical Success Factor.

1.6 Involvement, Commitment, and Sustained Payoffs

A strategic plan is futile if not used. When educators, citizens, parents, and learners don't feel they are part of planning, the results usually will be ignored or thwarted. And the planners grow frustrated seeing their product sit on shelves. Everyone—parents, teachers, principals, administrators, business members, board members, learners, citizens—has to be a part of strategic thinking and planning. In the next chapter, we will identify who should be partners in educational planning and thinking. We will see that the partners include the educational and societal stakeholders: those who will be affected by any changes and those who will effect them.

Our educational partners—learners, educators, and community members—must help with, and be a part of, strategic thinking and planning. The formal inclusion of all educational partners will help us to be responsive and responsible and to create a better future for tomorrow's child.

By asking and answering all seven questions (in Table 1.2), a practical and functional educational process emerges, as shown in Figure 1.4.

Based on societal payoffs, courses (which may be integrated with each other and additional learning experiences) may be developed and the resulting performance and mastery used to assist the learners and improve the system. This is different

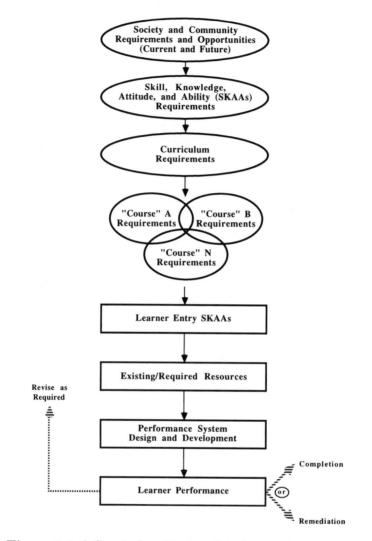

Figure 1.4. A Curriculum Design, Development, and Applications Sequence Based Upon Strategic Thinking

than the conventional approach, shown in Figure 1.5, which only pays lip service to Question 1 (in Table 1.2) and only delivers orthodox instruction resulting in "pass" or "fail" with no help to the struggling student or grist for system improvement.

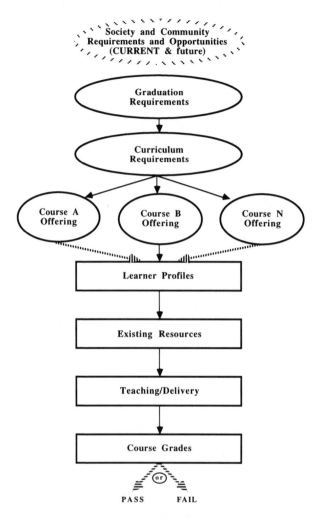

Figure 1.5. A Conventional Curriculum Design Process
NOTE: The learner can either pass or fail, and lessons learned from instruction and performance are not used to improve the content or curriculum.

Thinking and planning strategically can make the difference between repeating yesterday or capturing what works and changing what doesn't as we create a better tomorrow. This book identifies the whats and hows of successful strategic thinking and planning.

Key Terms

❏ *System.* The sum total of individual parts, working alone and together, to achieve a common purpose.

❏ *System approach to education.* Treating the entire educational enterprise as a system where a change in one part causes changes in all other parts; creates a total school system, not a system of schools.

❏ *Paradigm.* The boundary of a system and the set of ground rules that one uses to operate within that boundary.

❏ *Paradigm shift.* The situation where old boundaries and associated antique ground rules don't square with reality; they have shifted to a new reality where revised boundaries and ground rules are appropriate.

❏ *Comfort zone.* The areas (and stimuli) with which one feels unthreatened; the usual familiar territory where one's paradigm works well.

❏ *Ideal vision.* The preferred future in terms of the state of the world and conditions and quality of life for you, your organization, and your world; one useful criterion is to describe the world in which you want tomorrow's child to live.

❏ *Strategic thinking.* Knowing what to achieve, being able to justify the direction, and then finding the best ways to get there; being strategic is proactive and differs from being reactive to problems as they surface; strategic thinking is the most important product of strategic planning.

❏ *Mega-level thinking/planning.* Activity where the primary client and beneficiary of what gets planned and delivered is the society and community.

❏ *Macro-level thinking/planning.* Activity where the primary client and beneficiary of what gets planned and delivered is the school or educational system itself.

❏ *Micro-level thinking/planning.* Activity where the primary client and beneficiary of what gets planned and delivered is individuals and small groups within the school or system.

Notes

1. A *fanatic* may be defined as a person who redoubles his or her efforts after losing sight of the goals.

2. Regardless of the explanations offered in the literature for successions of these ebb-and-flow changes (Cuban, 1990), they all tend to overlook a common element: agreement on what education should de-

liver. If education "is the solution," what is the problem? I believe that one of the basic difficulties with delivering educational success is not in the dedication of principals, administrators, teachers, or parents but in the basic lack of definition and agreement on what are the objectives of education, what education should deliver. This book will deal extensively with how to fix this.

3. Rummler and Brache (1990) make a similar point, at the macro level, concerning private sector thinking.

4. Or do we only have to spend more money on education to be successful? Everyone who is convinced beyond a reasonable doubt that education's success can be assured by simply spending more money—even a lot more money—on it, go directly to Chapter 6.

5. This series is published by ChartHouse Learning Corporation, Burnsville, Minnesota.

6. Politicians are catching on. In *America 2000: An Education Strategy* (April 18, 1991), the U.S. president and secretary of education speak to the importance of thinking, competent learners who will make contributions to society. There is an increasing awareness that mindless learners being taught by frustrated teachers employing a rote and inappropriate curriculum will not suffice. It is interesting to note that this document, which intends to help education help society, provides goals for education but fails to link them either to an overall U.S. vision or to U.S. goals and objectives; caring alone is not enough.

7. I am aware that these are all useful ideas; it is only a warning that they might fail to deliver on their potential because we chose them for the wrong reasons. We have to match our means to useful ends.

2

A Framework and Basic Concepts for
Strategic Thinking and Planning

2.1 The Three Phases of Strategic
Thinking and Planning

This strategic planning model supplies a framework for defining useful and possibly new objectives. These objectives supply the bases for defining effective and efficient tactics. This framework applies to all educational levels. It has a number of functions (see Figure 2.1), starting with the commitment to the mega level of planning: The society is the primary client and beneficiary of what gets planned and delivered. This framework has three clusters: scoping, planning, and implementation and evaluation/continuous improvement.

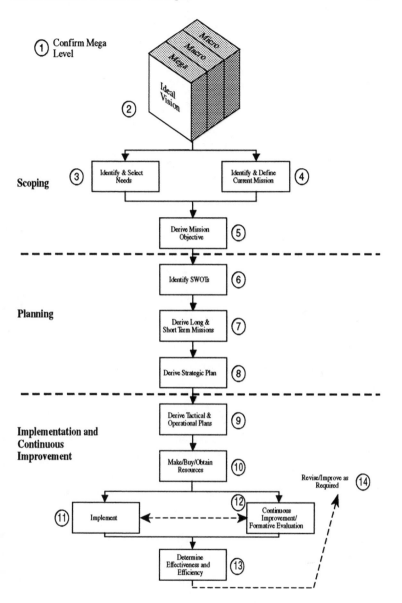

Figure 2.1. A Three-Cluster Strategic Planning Framework: Scoping, Planning, and Implementation and Evaluation/Continuous Improvement

The following describes the holistic and proactive strategic process.

A. *Scoping*

Confirm the mega level as the scope for being strategic: Step 1. Select the mega level where the primary client and beneficiary of what is planned and delivered is today's and tomorrow's society. The macro and micro levels are discouraged as the starting place. If you don't select the mega level, you assume that positive societal consequences will result! (See the questions in Table 1.2 and refer to Critical Success Factor 3 in Chapter 1.)

Identify the ideal vision: Step 2. Strategic planning defines and achieves a vision: the future we want for tomorrow's child. It is important to set an ideal vision *before* restricting oneself with unchallenged "educational philosophies" or "conventional wisdom." Although it is customary to initially identify values and beliefs as the starting place for strategic planning, I find that first defining the ideal vision allows planning partners to be unencumbered by premature adherence to unexamined values, or an "educational philosophy." In practice, beliefs and values are considered when developing the ideal vision. Actually, "philosophy" usually deals with means, not ends; strategic thinking and planning focuses on results before selecting the means.

Strategic planning, in its most powerful form, identifies results based upon an ideal vision: a mega-level "dream" (Kaufman, 1992a, 1992b). Just as Martin Luther King, Jr. had a dream, and Walt Disney noted that if you have a dream you can achieve it, we should develop our dream upon which to derive our educational objectives—our ideal vision. The ideal vision *is* the ideal: In what kind of world do we want our grandchildren to live? From this ideal, we select stepping-stone objectives to move us from current results ever closer to the ideal. We construct a results ladder that will link our three levels of results (Figure 2.2).

Planners having initial discomfort with addressing societal outcomes—the mega level—often ignore or assume them. If

Figure 2.2. The Ladder Formed by the Results at the Micro, Macro, and Mega Levels, Where the Results and Consequences at All Levels Interrelate

they do, so-called strategic planning actually stops at short-term stop-gap objectives and a true strategic plan is never developed or accomplished. Instead of first defining the vision of the world in which we want tomorrow's child to live, attention is immediately diverted to courses and subject matter assuming that societally useful results will follow (such as is shown in Figure 1.5 in Chapter 1).

> *Critical Success Factor 4*: Use an ideal vision as the underlying basis for planning (don't limit yourself to one just for your organization).

Although some (using out-of-date paradigms) will dismiss developing an ideal vision as academic, realize that without an ideal vision we limit thinking and planning to reactive, quick-fix tactics. Deriving a shared ideal vision is so important that several other authors have also identified it as basic to contemporary thinking and survival. With a shared ideal vision, each person can know how to contribute, in their unique way, to that journey. We use it as a North Star for guidance and steering.

A shared ideal vision is best when societally related. A vision should not be at the macro level and merely focused on the organization (e.g., have the state's highest college placement). Simply striving to beat the competition (e.g., outperforming area private schools) is transitory and does not obtain commitment to continuous improvement toward a societally useful destination.

Ideal visions targeting a common "perfect" destination allow alignment among the society, the organization, and the aspirations of all organizational members. This concept is increasingly encouraged. Senge (1990) quotes several "practical" executives on the importance of generating and using an ideal vision to drive all organizational contributions. For example, he quotes Kazuo Inamori of the Kyocera Corporation as urging people to "look inward" to aim for perfection, not simply being the best: an intrinsic and not an extrinsic vision.

If we want a world at peace (e.g., no deaths from war, no deaths or disabilities from drug addiction, no crime), those should form the ideal vision. Issues of "practicality" should not be considered here (otherwise we would limit ourselves to that which we are currently achieving or know we can deliver). If we don't reach for a better future through strategic planning, how will we ever know the directions for the first step? Cynics will carp about these being "utopian" or "not real world." Forgive them. We must set an ideal standard, even if we never get there, so that we know what direction in which to move and plot our continuous progress.

Beliefs, values, and wishes—the "mental filters" through which education and the world are viewed—drive the ways partners address planning. They are usually strongly held and unexamined. (Some people call these their "philosophy.") Beliefs and values are identified and agreed upon as they are considered when deriving the ideal vision. By judging beliefs and values in the context of societally useful results, they are open for reconsideration.

The success of strategic planning and what education will deliver may hinge on the planning partners' abilities to adopt new philosophies, frames of reference, and basic beliefs about people. With an openly derived ideal vision, previously unchallenged beliefs and values will likely be tempered and reevaluated by the planners as they shift from a means orientation to identification of the kind of world we want to help create.

Identify needs: Step 3. By defining a "need" as a gap in results (more on this in Chapter 3) and employing available sources of needs information (including performance and perceptions), the gaps between the ideal vision and current results and consequences are determined. Not only are the gaps between current and ideal status harvested but also the gaps that will exist in each of the nearer-term years (2010, 2000, 1998, next year, this year). Future trends and opportunities are also identified and documented (c.f., Naisbitt & Aburdene, 1990; Toffler, 1990). History is also important: how we got to where we are now (so we learn from the past).

Identify the current mission: Step 4. At the same time as doing steps 2 and 3, the current mission statement is obtained and (as is usually necessary) rewritten in results terms.

Derive Mission Objective: Step 5. The mission objective states where the organization is headed and includes the rigorous criteria by which to precisely determine the extent to which success has been achieved.

The mission objective considers the matches and mismatches among the ideal vision, needs, and current mission (Steps 2, 3, 4). The planners find the portions that are shared and those that differ. Reconcile differences among these and find the collective ground: Negotiate to deliver what is right, not just what is acceptable. When disagreements linger, collect missing data to define the gaps in results among the ideal vision, needs, and existing mission. An ends focus is vital.

From the mission objective, tactical (ways and means to achieve desired results) objectives may be derived. By aligning with an ideal vision, methods, means, and resources may be both sensibly selected and justified.

Relating strategic objectives to our ideal vision moves us continuously toward creating the world in which we want future generations to live. Based on this, we may sensibly create a responsive educational system. This mega commitment defines a better future and discourages a drift in the same directions we are now heading. Because the organizational mission for education, the macro level, rolls down and is derived from the ideal vision, it identifies those portions of the ideal vision that it commits to deliver, as shown in Figure 2.3.

This step delivers a mission objective ("where we are headed" plus "how we will know when we have arrived"). Needs are prioritized on the basis of the costs to close the gap versus the costs of ignoring it. The key is to prepare measurable performance indicators skillfully and select the appropriate level of results for writing mission objectives.

B. *Planning*

Identify SWOTs (strengths, weaknesses, opportunities, and threats): Step 6. While uncovering the system's strengths, weaknesses, opportunities, and threats, don't leave out or gloss over any of the SWOTs. Be objective.

Derive the long- and short-term missions: Step 7. Based upon the products of steps 1-6, select building-block missions—macro-level objectives—for the long term (e.g., for 2010) and closer-in objectives (e.g., 2000, 1998). Figure 2.4 shows the relationship between an ideal vision (or preferred future) and the closer-in strategic objectives.

Develop strategic plan: Step 8. Based on previous steps, the product of this step provides the basis for answering the key questions: What? Why? When? so that justifiable decisions may be made about How? Who? When? and Where?

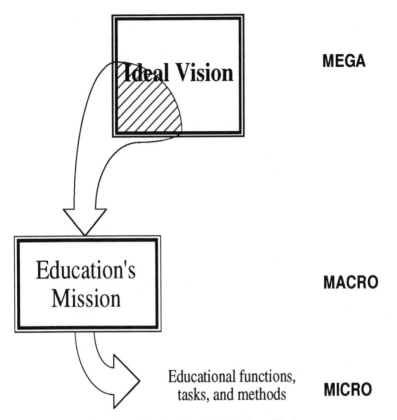

Figure 2.3. Missions Derive From the Ideal Vision
NOTE: An educational agency will select what portion of the ideal vision it commits to address. The relationship among Mega, Macro, and Micro are shown.

c. *Implementation and Evaluation / Continuous Improvement*

Derive tactical and operational plan: Step 9. Operational, or in-process, milestones for implementation are set along with the identification and selection of the tactics, methods, and means to be used, all based on the previous results.

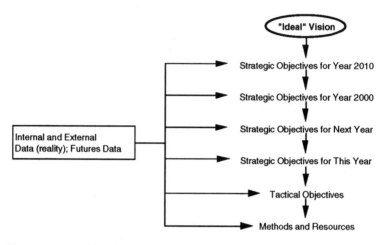

Figure 2.4. The Relationship Between an Ideal Vision (even though we might not expect to get there in our lifetime or our children's lifetime) and Related, Closer-In Strategies
SOURCE: Based on Kaufman, Herman, and Watters (in press); used with permission.

Put the strategic plan to work and revise as required: Steps 10-14. The activities and the results of these last steps include (a) making/buying/obtaining/designing and developing the responses; (b) implementing what has been planned; (c) conducting formative evaluation and continuous improvement for revising anything and everything as required during implementation; and finally, (d) determining effectiveness and efficiency.

This last phase also includes summative evaluation, where purposes are compared with final results. Based upon the evaluation—comparing results with intentions— decisions are made about what to continue and what to revise.

Strategic planning is a continuing process. It is a way of thinking and a process for deriving practical and justifiable plans. By taking a mega perspective, the linkages—a chain of results, means, and resources—will be demonstrated and accomplished (see Figure 2.5).

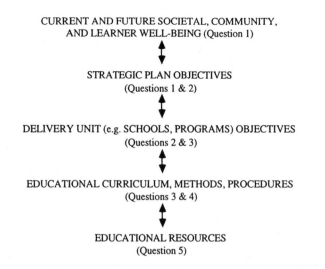

Figure 2.5. The Chain of Educational Results (and means), With the Basic Strategic Questions (Table 1.2) They Ask and Answer

2.2 Mistakes Usually Made by Educators and Their Partners

Like their private sector counterparts, educators consistently make a number of mistakes. Avoiding them could mean the difference between just another planning document that gathers dust on distant shelves and a revitalized educational system.

Planning at the course or program level, not at the societal—mega—level. Education is charged to provide learners with the abilities to be successful and contributing citizens. If we don't define future societal success, then we are assuming that all our courses and activities will be useful. How successful is our current curriculum and educational system? Can it simply be patched and mended by adding a course here, tougher requirements there?

Not using an ideal vision because doing so is "imprac-tical." This argument goes something like this: "'They' will laugh at us if we aren't practical! And if they ridicule us, we won't get anything done!" The argument continues, "We all know there isn't enough money, and there never will be." Finally, they add, "A 5-year planning horizon is far enough—let's not get all academic."

These are classic "cop-outs": an attempt to avoid setting distant purposes in fear that someone will try to hold the planners and educators accountable for not getting there. It also ignores the fact that the ideal vision is not the same as the mission objective. The ideal vision first sets the *destination* toward which all strategic and tactical planning will head. If we don't set the ideal vision—the preferred distant future—we won't know which way to head, and we also will limit ourselves to what we think we can get done based on today's realities. Without a dream, we only have the here and now, and most of us agree that is unacceptable. A person's reach exceeds his or her grasp, and an ideal vision should stretch our intentions beyond today's unimpressive realities. Simply increasing our efficiency in what we are now doing is counterproductive: You cannot solve today's problems with the same paradigms, tools, and methods which created them.

Preparing objectives in terms of means, not results. Objectives tell us where to go and how to know when we have arrived. If we only set our sights on processes (using computers) or resources (higher wages, more teachers), we put the educational-methods cart before the expected-results horse.

A variation on this is *selecting solutions before identifying destinations.* Just about every activist group, good or bad, has a favorite solution or quick fix. Resist picking a solution (or resource or method) until you know where you are headed and why.

Developing a plan without the input of representative educational partners. Although a plan will be put together more quickly when done by a small group, the product is not likely to be accepted by others who feel they have not contributed. In addition, included partners will be able to contribute to the plan and thus make it both better and representative.

Setting objectives based solely upon the perceptions of the planning partners and not also being anchored in performance realities. Although people know what they want, they don't always know what they should have. They also don't know much about gaps between current results and required ones. Provide planning partners with the realities of future trends, opportunities, and consequences.

Skipping some of the steps of strategic planning. Although there are a number of steps, leaving out even one will diminish the quality and usefulness of the plan. Review the model (Figure 2.1) and the seven basic strategic questions (Table 1.2). Which steps and questions can really be omitted?

Assuming that all strategic planning approaches (a) are basically the same and/or (b) are nothing but common sense/intuition. All models aren't the same. Most are reactive, *and* start at too low a level. Most plans deliberately attempt to improve courses, or increase graduation rates, but assume they will turn out learners who will be successful citizens. If intuition were enough, the schools would already be wonderful.

Trying to get planning done too quickly. There is a fine balancing act to strategic planning. One temptation is to believe that the concepts, or the success factors, are straightforward and obvious, or thinking that, by simply presenting them to the planning partners, it will only take a little discussion and the planning partners will understand and accept them. People, especially implementers, often find it difficult to give up process-oriented thinking and territorial imperatives. They tend to stay within their comfort zones. Provide plenty of examples and assurances before moving forward. Take enough time to let the planning partners work through both the concepts and the implications.

2.3 Implied Criticism When Doing Strategic Thinking and Planning

Any time you start an intervention, such as being strategic, many people mistakenly take the activity as an implied criticism (Kaufman, 1989). After all, if you want to change things, or even offer that possibility, it might signal that the status quo is not good enough. Just the implication is enough to make some education partners very nervous (threatened, in fact). This implied criticism frequently results in an attack on the strategic planners, the planning team, associated consultants—in fact, anyone involved with the effort. Surface the possibility of unintended criticism very early in the planning and deal with it openly and honestly. Recall (Table 1.5) that bringing up issues such as who is to be the primary client and beneficiary of what gets planned and delivered might jar some people's comfort zones. Be patient and helpful. Assist others in seeing how to contribute toward what first attracted them to education: to help learners be successful.

Show by word and deed that strategic thinking and planning are not abusive, fault finding, blame placing, or disparaging. They are empowering. By asking important partners to help determine the future, they become partners in useful change, not victims of reacting to change.

2.4 Educational Results, Efforts, Consequences, and Payoffs

A useful guide to use in relating what your educational organization uses, does, and delivers is a five-unit framework called the OEM: the Organizational Elements Model (Kaufman, 1988b, 1992b). The OEM identifies three types of results (one for the mega level, another for the macro, and a third for the micro) and two types of means and resources. Any educational organization may be described as using and relating these five elements. Table 2.1 shows the five elements of inputs, processes, products, outputs, and outcomes along with some examples of each.

TABLE 2.1 The Organizational Elements Model (OEM) and an Educational Example of Each

	INPUTS (resources, ingredients)	PROCESSES (how-to's; means; methods; procedures)	PRODUCTS (en route --building-block-- results)	OUTPUTS (the aggregated products of the system that are delivered or deliverable to society)	OUTCOMES (the contributions of outputs in and for society and the community)
ORGANIZATIONAL LEVEL					
EXAMPLES	Existing personnel; identified needs, goals, objectives, policies, regulations, laws, money, values, and societal and community characteristics; current quality of life, learner entry characteristics, teacher competencies, buildings, equipment, etc.	Total quality management - continuous improvement; teaching; learning; in-service training, managing, accelerated learning; site-based managing; accountability; etc.	Course completed; competency test passed; skill acquired; learner accomplishments; instructor accomplishments; etc.	Graduates; completers; dropouts; job placements; certified licensees; etc.	Self-sufficient, self reliant, productive individual who is socially competent and effective, contributing to self and others; no addiction to others or to substances; financially independent; continued funding of agency; etc.
CLUSTER	EFFORTS		RESULTS		SOCIETAL RESULTS/IMPACT
SCOPE		INTERNAL (Organizational)			EXTERNAL (Societal)
PLANNING LEVEL			MICRO	MACRO	MEGA
PRIMARY CLIENT OR BENEFICIARY			INDIVIDUAL OR SMALL GROUP	SCHOOL SYSTEM OR SCHOOL	SOCIETY/COMMUNITY
STRATEGIC QUESTION			Do you care about the specific skills, knowledges, attitudes, and abilities of the learners as they move from course to course, and level to level?	Do you care about the quality -competence- of the completers and leavers when they leave your educational system?	Do you care about the success of learners after they leave your educational system and are citizens?

NOTE: Based in part on Kaufman and Herman (1991b) and Kaufman (1988b).

The organizational elements relate to the levels and scale of planning: Outcomes are results at the mega level; outputs are results at the macro level; products are results at the micro level.

The OEM provides a template, or pattern, to identify the results and resources any organization uses and delivers: Outcomes are external (mega) results in and for society; outputs and products are within-the-educational system results; processes are the ways and means for getting results; and inputs are the ingredients we can or must use.

When being strategic, all of the organizational elements must be integrated and linked. For example, the existing facilities, teachers, and learning resources (inputs) may be used in delivering learning opportunities/teaching (processes). These, together, should deliver mastery in courses and proficiency in the application of principles, values, and decisioning (products) that, when gathered together, lead to graduation or certification (outputs). All of the internal organizational elements—inputs, processes, products, outputs—can and should deliver people who are self-sufficient, self-reliant, mutually contributing citizens of today and tomorrow (outcomes). The relationships among the organizational elements, levels of planning, emphases, and typical examples are shown in Table 2.1.

When thinking and planning strategically, we start with the outcomes (mega-level results) we desire and then identify the internal elements (outputs, products, processes, and inputs) that will deliver those. The educational system's success is based on how well educational resources contribute to useful processes, and those must deliver successful en route mastery for graduation and citizenship. This chain of results that links educational resources, interventions, and the three levels of results may be shown in "shorthand" using the terms from the OEM and noting the three levels of educational planning (Figure 2.6).

It is important that all of the organizational elements are integrated. Education is a system, and all parts must work independently and together if success is to be defined and delivered.

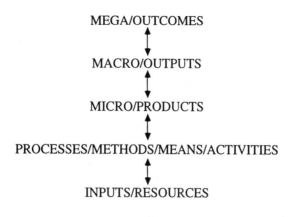

Figure 2.6. The Educational Results (and means) Chain
SOURCE: Based on Kaufman, Herman, and Watters (in press) and
Kaufman (1988b, 1992b).
NOTE: If the relationships (shown by arrows) become blurred or poorly
linked, the system "vibrates" and becomes inefficient and ineffective.

2.5 Strategic Planning and
Strategic Planning Plus

Strategic planning defines *what* educational results we should
deliver to meet current and predicted opportunities, problems,
and conditions. Tactical planning defines *how* we can best deliver the required educational results. *Strategic Planning Plus*
(Kaufman, 1992b) extends conventional strategic planning and
tactical planning by *also* identifying the kind of future we want
to create while taking care of today's housekeeping problems.
Strategic Planning Plus (SP+) adds the mega level to traditional
strategic planning.

Although most conventional approaches think and plan on
the basis of the educational organization itself as the primary
client and beneficiary, SP+ intends to identify and achieve a different future. It does not simply react to externally imposed
problems and restraints. SP+ intends to identify and create the
kind of world in which we want tomorrow's child to live. Conventional strategic planning primarily reacts to trends, issues,
politics, and projected realities.

Strategic thinking and planning, in its most powerful application, are proactive and positive. They do not settle for the here and now.

The role of needs assessment is important to mention here but will be addressed in detail later in the book. A needs assessment identifies the gaps between current and desired results. It prioritizes them and selects the most important for closure. Because needs relate to gaps in results, a needs assessment will identify gaps at the mega/outcome level as well as at the macro/output and micro/product levels. This way, all levels of the results chain—all elements of the OEM—will be related. There will be much more on needs assessment in Chapter 3.

2.6 Partners in Educational Thinking, Planning, and Success

Education does not live by curriculum alone. In a democracy, the agencies that serve the public must obtain their agreement concerning what the educational system is to deliver, who will be the recipients, and what supporting resources may be expected. Shared ownership of the educational enterprise is not only sensible, it is vital (Drucker, 1973).

The selection of the planning partners must assure that key perspectives, understandings, values, and constituencies contribute to identifying the ideal vision/preferred future as well as developing and/or approving of the system's mission objectives. When identifying and selecting the educational planning partners, assure they are typical emissaries of their constituencies. If ethnic, or age, composition is important—and they usually are—obtain a representative sample. Scan the demographics of your system and service area and make certain that no group is left out.

Individual representatives should exemplify at least three clusters:

- learners (at all levels);
- educators (teachers, principals, administrators, staff); and
- community members (including parents).

Typically, a stratified random sample of each constituency-based partner group will furnish representativeness. Do not create huge groups, just include those who exemplify the individuals and clients the planned changes are supposed to serve. Do not include "tokens" or pack the planning group with friends.

The planning partners will supply judgments concerning an ideal vision and will usually help (or at least approve) mission objectives based on that preferred future. As planning proceeds (as described in later chapters), they will also supply perceptions of the educational and societal needs and prioritize them on the basis of the costs to meet the needs versus the costs of ignoring them. The Critical Success Factors can serve as guides for strategic thinking and planning and will also serve as reminders of the basic elements for success.

It isn't enough to identify the partners, get them to be active contributors as well. Obtain acceptance of the mega planning level: the most practical. By familiarizing the partners with the optional levels and the advantages and disadvantages of each, you allow them an informed choice. It is important that all partners agree on the scope of the strategic thinking and planning, have common understandings and expectations as they develop the ideal vision, and derive (or endorse) the mission objectives. If there are disagreements, they usually come from arguments over means, not ends. Reconciling differences is usually straightforward when (a) there is a firm emphasis on ends, and not means; (b) assuring that the ideal vision and the educational mission objective are targeted to the mega level; and (c) all involved understand their own comfort zones and how they might limit themselves from seeing new vistas and approaches.

The partners will not only set the level and scope of planning, they will become the advocates for societally useful change. The importance of involvement and commitment should be obvious. Without the educational partners agreeing and supporting the vision and mission of the educational system, quick fixes and attacks from outside are likely to deflect the whole adventure. Together, educators, learners, and community members can make education both useful and cost-effective.

Key Terms

❏ *Strategic planning.* A process for defining useful (and possible new and additional) objectives and their linkage to effective and efficient tactics. The model offered here has three phases: scoping, planning, and implementation and evaluation/continuous improvement; this differs from usual planning approaches that assume current objectives as useful and valid and tend to react to existing problems.

❏ *Need.* At least for rational planning, the gap between current and desired/required results.

❏ *Mission statement.* Where one is headed: the destination.

❏ *Mission objective.* A mission statement plus the criteria for measuring when one has (or has not) arrived.

❏ *SWOTs.* Strengths, weaknesses, opportunities, and threats.

❏ *Organizational Elements Model (OEM).* The elements that make up that which every organization uses (inputs), does (processes), accomplishes (products), delivers (outputs) outside of itself, plus the external consequences of all of it (outcomes) in and for society; results at the micro level are products; those at the macro level are outputs; and those at the mega level are outcomes.

❏ *Strategic Planning Plus (SP+).* An approach that extends conventional strategic planning and tactical planning by *also* identifying the kind of future we want to create for tomorrow's child (mega-level results) while also taking care of today's housekeeping problems.

❏ *Needs assessment.* The process of identifying gaps in results (needs), placing them in priority order, and selecting the most important for reduction or elimination.

3

Objectives and Needs Assessment: Basic Building Blocks

Being strategic is simple—once the shift from conventional wisdom (which got us to were we are now) to "thinking results and societal good" is made. Earlier chapters provided the umbrella concepts, including a strategic thinking/planning framework and its related steps, the three levels of planning, and the elements of building a partnership. This chapter provides additional, more focused, building blocks and summarizes the six Critical Success Factors for being strategic.

It would be nice if there were but one or two simple "secrets" to strategic thinking, but that is not the case. Adding to one philosopher's observation, "for every problem there is one solution that is simple, straightforward, understandable, acceptable to everyone, and wrong." Here is the balance of the must-know basics.

3.1 We Don't Like Complexity

We have a burning desire to simplify, reduce, condense. Our world, thanks to television, has become a series of sound bites. We expect instant results. But not everything is simple or instantaneous. As nice as that would be, the world doesn't work that way. People, including learners, are unique and complex, and so too is society. An educational system that intends to help learners be successful in, and contribute to, society is also diverse and complex. If education and life were amenable to simple checklists and one-size-fits-all formulas, we wouldn't have any problems today.

Strategic thinking and planning must take advantage of this rich complexity and provide an approach and results that improve the world of our learners and educational partners. Following are some useful, and important, terms and tools. They are as uncomplicated, and yet as valid, as I know how to make them.

3.2 On Thinking (and Talking) Straight in Education

Critical Success Factor 1 encourages us to be open to new ways of viewing and dealing with education. Critical Success Factor 2 shows us the most important way to be precise in thinking and talking: Differentiate between ends and means. Critical Success Factor 3 adds more precision: Act on the basis of three levels of planning and results—mega/outcomes, macro/outputs, micro/products. Other concepts and tools for thinking and talking straight are ahead in this chapter, including

- the difference between objectives and goals;
- the relationship between a mission statement and a mission objective;
- defining "need" as a gap in results;
- the differences among needs assessment, needs analysis, front-end analysis, and the so-called training needs assessment; and
- the planning requirement that we not only identify and select needs—gaps in results—to close but that we also maintain what is working as well as identify opportunities.

3.3 Preparing Useful Objectives

A. *A Focus on Ends, Not Means*

Where are we going? How do we know when we have arrived? Mager (1975) set the standard by identifying that an objective should state, without confusion,

(a) what performance is to be demonstrated,
(b) who or what will demonstrate that performance,
(c) under what conditions the performance will be observed, and
(d) what criteria will be used to determine success.

Good advice: Objectives don't state *how* we will achieve the result, only what performance will be exhibited, by whom or what will it be demonstrated, where it will be shown, and what we will use to measure it. Thus we address ends, not means, as in Critical Success Factor 2.

B. *As Easy as ABCD*[1]

Table 3.1 shows a format for preparing "Mager-type" objectives, built on ABCD. Table 3.2 provides a hypothetical example of an objective using the ABCD elements.

TABLE 3.1 A Format for Preparing Measurable Objectives: As Easy as ABCD

A: Who or what is the Ⓐudience, target, or recipient?

B: What Ⓑehavior, performance, accomplishment, end, or result is to be demonstrated?

C: Under what Ⓒonditions will the behavior or accomplishment be observed?

D: What Ⓓata--criteria, ideally measured on an interval or ratio scale--will be used to calibrate success?

c. Aren't There Some Things That Just Are Not Measurable?

There is a very simple answer to this commonly held proposition: No! In fact, everything is measurable and measurable on a mathematical scale (Kaufman, 1972, 1991c; Stevens, 1951).

Table 3.3 presents a taxonomy of results, which shows that even naming (a nominal scale) is measurement. If we can name it, we are measuring it, and there are statistics for handling that type of data (chi-square, for instance).

Sometimes we don't know enough about a phenomenon (such as self-esteem or locus of control) to develop true interval or ratio scale measures, so we simply write goals, or purposes. When we do know enough about a phenomenon to write true objectives (an interval or ratio scale), then ethically we should do so.

TABLE 3.2 A Sample Completed ABCD Form

	A Format for Preparing Measurable Objectives: As Easy as ABCD	
	ABCD Element	**Hypothetical Objective**
A:	Who or what is the <u>A</u>udience, target, or recipient?	100% of all learners, completers, and leavers who enrolled at the English-Steffy Unified School District after September 1, 1992.
B:	What <u>B</u>ehavior, performance, accomplishment, end, or result is to be demonstrated?	Will be accepted to postsecondary education, and/or get and keep a job that pays at least as much as it costs them to live. None will dropout without meeting state requirements, and all will be self-sufficient.
C:	Under what <u>C</u>onditions will the behavior or accomplishment be observed?	Both in school and beyond exit: Each year, there will be an independent audit of in-school registrations and district records, as well as an independent placement and follow-up study of all completers and leavers.
D:	What <u>D</u>ata--criteria, ideally measured on an interval or ratio scale--will be used to calibrate success?	There will be 0 unapproved dropouts, and 0 previously enrolled learners who did not get accepted to a postsecondary program accredited by a regional education commision and/or who did not get and keep a job for at least 6 months (barring seasonal or economic layoffs) as reported and certified by the superintendent.

TABLE 3.3 A Taxonomy of Educational Results

TYPE OF RESULT	DESCRIPTION/LABEL	SCALE OF MEASUREMENT
Naming	Goal, Aim, Purpose	NOMINAL
Rank Order		ORDINAL
Equal scale distances with arbitrary zero point	Objective, Performance Indicator, Performance Criteria	INTERVAL
Equal scale distances with know zero point		RATIO

SOURCE: Based, in part, on Kaufman (1972, 1988b, 1992b), and Kaufman, Herman, and Watters (in press).

Everything *is* measurable. The only differences are in the reliability of the measurement: Interval and ratio scale measures are much more reliable than nominal or ordinal scales. But pretending that some things are not measurable, or "intangible," avoids reality and places important—and often very humanistic—results and achievements in question.

3.4 Preparing Mission Statements and Mission Objectives

Objectives at all levels—mega, macro, and micro—can and should include all of the elements highlighted in the ABCD format. Frequently, objectives for the entire educational organization only deal with intentions and thus are best called "mission statements." As we will discuss at greater length in the next chapter, we should prepare mission objectives and not be content with motivational statements of intent, such as "education for all" or even "educational excellence for all learners."

Although a mission statement ("achieving quality," "excellence in teaching," "develop each child to his or her greatest potential") sets a direction, it is hardly the stuff for strategic thinking, let alone strategic planning. We must, if we are serious about getting useful results, state both where we are going and how we can measure (on an interval or ratio scale) when we have arrived:

mission statement + measurable criteria = mission objective

The differences among objectives are only in terms of level, not in substance or content. This is so important that it is Critical Success Factor 5:

Critical Success Factor 5: Prepare all objectives—including mission objectives—to include precise, clear statements of *both* where you are going and how will you know when you have arrived.

An algorithm for preparing any objective is provided in Figure 1.2.

3.5 Define "Needs" as Gaps in Results, Not as Insufficient Levels of Resources or Methods

As noted in Chapters 1 and 2, the word *need* is all too often used (in both planning and everyday life) as a verb. When we use *need* as a verb, we are prescribing—imposing—a solution, method, procedure, or activity. So ingrained in our common language is *need* as a verb that we are always prescribing to others how they should do things, what they should use, and the way they should live their lives.

When planning (and indeed in one's own personal life), using *need* as a noun—a gap between current results and desired ones—can make the difference between success and failure. As we noted in Chapter 1, many educational reforms have been solutions in search of problems: means prescribed in the hope of delivering useful ends. Just as Critical Success Factor 2 emphasizes the important difference between ends and means, and Critical Success Factor 3 extends that difference to recognize that there are three levels of ends, or results, the use of *need* to denote a gap in results is also vital to strategic thinking and planning.

Critical Success Factor 6: Need is a gap between current results and desired or required ones (not a gap in resources or methods and means).

By reserving the use of *need* to signify a gap in results, as shown in Figure 3.1, your strategic thinking and planning will yield a firm basis for identifying and selecting useful ends and then finding the best means to get there. By so doing, you will avoid rushing from unwarranted assumptions (we "need" more computers; we "need" more in-service training) to foregone conclusions ("computers will make learners more competent in both school and life"; "in-service training will make teachers competent and successful"). When we choose to use *need* as a noun, we benefit by putting Critical Success Factors 1, 2, and 3 to work.

A. *Words: You Change, but Not Me*

Unfortunately, as educators, we are happy enough to develop change programs for learners but tend to resist change ourselves. We struggle mightily to stay within our existing comfort zones. The use of the word *need* is a case in point. We teach our youngsters to be precise in word and deed, and instructors model this rigor. We don't allow kids to use slang, racial or ethnic slurs, or sexist terminology. Although it was once conventional to use *he* for both genders, we now realize that doing so diminishes the distinction between females and males. We don't call women "girls" because it carries a subtle meta message that they cannot be responsible as independent adults.

But wait: When it is suggested that *need* be used only as a noun—the gap between current results and desired ones—the conversation often turns hostile: "I know what I mean, and so does everyone else!" "Stop quibbling over semantics." "Don't *you* tell me what to say." Even after intellectually convincing someone that not using *need* as a verb (or in the verb sense)—such as "need to," "need for," "needing," or "needed"—is a useful way to make certain we don't select a means before defining the gap in ends to be closed, the old "using-*need*-as-a-verb" behavior continues. Old habits and antique paradigms die hard.

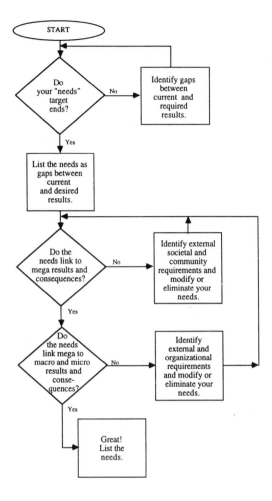

Figure 3.1. An Algorithm for Relating Needs to Gaps in Results and Also Assuring That They Link All Three Levels of Results

B. *Differentiating Between Ends and Means*

Relating ends and means while not confusing them will become increasingly important as we move through this applications guide to strategic thinking. It will reappear again when we address writing useful mission objectives, preparing worthwhile performance indicators, and assessing needs.

3.6 Applications of Needs Assessment

In Chapters 4, 5, and 6, we will have more illustrations of the importance of Critical Success Factor 5, for needs assessment is the linchpin between strategic thinking (scoping) and strategic planning. If we haven't identified the correct gaps in results—needs—how can we ever select the most effective and efficient means to achieve required results? Needs and related solutions and resources allow us to move more surely from quick fixes to sustained success.

Needs assessment is the process that

(a) *identifies* gaps between current results and desired ones,
(b) *prioritizes* the gaps in results (needs), and
(c) *selects* the most important needs for closure or reduction.

By defining needs as gaps in results, we may identify and design responsive and responsible educational systems. The most rational way of selecting means (programs, projects, organizational structures) is on the basis of getting from current results to desired ones.

A. *Collect Needs Data at All Three Levels*

Needs may be identified at all three levels of the organization: mega, macro, and micro. Needs assessments, regardless of the level, will identify the gaps in results, prioritize them, and allow you to select the most important for closure based on criticality.

Needs data come from

- perceptions and personal experiences, called "soft" (or "sensing") data because they are private and not independently verifiable, and
- independently verifiable performance results, called "hard" data.

Both types of data are indispensable. Sensed, or "soft," data-based needs provide perceived reality and sensitivity to issues of values and preferences. They also may reveal observations concerning the methods and procedures that led to the currently undesired results, which will help us when we later select ways and means to meet needs. But feelings alone are not enough.

Data concerning gaps in performance are required. These independently verifiable needs may be both in human and in organizational performance. Such data are termed "hard" because they derive from actual observed performance. Hard data might include external results (outcomes) such as graduates who are successful in life, school image, drug-related death rates, numbers of people with positive credit ratings, quality of community life, and the like.

Hard data also might include internal organizational performance indicators (outputs and products) such as productivity of teachers, failure rates, counselor case completions, absenteeism, morale, school climate, delivered services, and complaints.

Treat the performance-based data as equally important as the soft data. They supply additional facts for identifying, documenting, and selecting needs. Together, the sensed needs plus the performance-based data provide the needs assessment data. Depending on the needs assessment level selected, collect external and/or internal data.

B. *Data Sources for Needs Assessment*

When collecting data, look at two information sources: the perceptions of the planning partners and actual performance discrepancies collected from objective observations. You may collect partners' perceptions concerning performance discrepancies—needs sensing—by using a variety of tools and methods ranging from face-to-face meetings to remote data collection methods including rating scales, questionnaires, the Delphi technique, nominal group technique, structured interviews, or written assessments. Be sure to collect both hard and soft data. Needs assessments are more than just questionnaires.

In designing or selecting needs sensing data collection instruments, be sure the correct questions are asked and that they are created without bias. Make certain the questions focus responses on results, not resources (inputs) or methods and techniques (processes). The questions should be comprehensive, covering the range of needs, without imposing on the respondents with long and/or complex issues and queries. The instruments must be both valid (measuring what they really are supposed to measure) and reliable (measuring it consistently).

Collecting internal organizational performance data is easy. Most schools and systems have a lot of hard data. You only have to decide what you want and then find it. Useful data points might include truancy, contact hours, graduation rates, disciplinary actions, problem referrals, audit exceptions, ethics violations, accidents, on-site injuries, grievances, courses completed, certified competencies, sick leave, work samples, and rejection rates. Assure the validity and reliability of these data, and use them only when they will supply useful performance information.

Because the planning partners have agreed on the mega needs assessment level, collect external performance data. Some examples include successful graduate/completer, recidivism, civil rights adjudications, arrests and convictions, performance and success. Include parents, citizens, and workers as "soft" data sources, including the educational partners' perceptions of their satisfaction.

A format for listing and summarizing needs as they are identified is provided in Table 3.4. By using it, needs can be recorded systematically. By identifying the current and desired results, as well as possible means, any planning partner who seems insistent about a favored means (computers, arts, physical education) can see it listed in the "Possible Means" column and realize that the entry will stay there until a related gap in results is identified.

c. Using Needs Assessment Data to Justify Budgets, Resources, and Methods

One educational frustration is that there never seems to be enough money to fund activities. It seems as if our pockets are always empty, and we have to scrimp, save, and scrounge to keep the enterprise on track. There are a number of ways to reach worthy destinations when resources are scarce:

TABLE 3.4 Needs Assessment Summary Format

Current Results	Possible Means	Required Results	Ideal Vision Element	Need Level		
				Micro	Macro	Mega

1. Cut fat.
2. Move from high-labor-intensive delivery of education to alternative (and often technology-based) delivery methods.
3. Find the money.

And, if all of this fails:

4. Cut vital programs and services.

Option 1 should be the first on our to-do list. Option 2 should continue to interest us; our future educational success seems to depend upon it. Cutting muscle and bone, option 4, must be avoided. So, if you have cut the fat, and have gotten more efficient in the design and delivery of learning opportunities, how do you get the money?

Value added—the extent to which we recover costs and deliver beyond the break-even point—is becoming high on citizens' and legislators' lists of criteria, as well it should. Why not get a positive return on our educational investments? The way to convince others that what you want to do should be supported is to document the gaps in results (needs), identify the best ways and means to close those gaps, and also demonstrate what it costs to meet the need as compared with what it costs to ignore it. Needs assessments are vital in making any rational decision.

D. *Needs Assessment and the Organizational Elements Model*

In Chapter 2, the Organization Elements Model (OEM) was introduced as a template, or pattern, for relating that which educational organizations use (inputs), do (processes), produce (products), deliver (outputs), and affect in society (outcomes). In addition, the definition of a need as a gap in results has been continually emphasized. Now, we can show the relationship between the OEM, needs, and needs assessments. Figure 3.2 shows the OEM, the three types of results, and the three varieties of needs as open arrows. Also, quasi needs—gaps in inputs and/or products—are shown as shaded arrows.

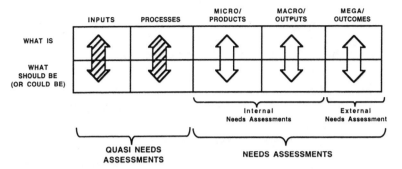

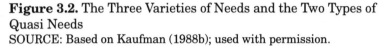

Figure 3.2. The Three Varieties of Needs and the Two Types of Quasi Needs
SOURCE: Based on Kaufman (1988b); used with permission.

The OEM can help us visualize and relate what our educational organization uses, does, delivers, and contributes, then compare these against what it should use, do, deliver, and contribute: the gaps between "what is" and "what should (or could) be." Use the OEM for your school or system, and you will see how things relate as well as the missing or nonintegrating elements.

E. Quasi Needs Are Gaps in Resources or "How-To's"

As noted earlier, we are usually eager to get education moving, quickly. Although it is tempting to talk about "in-service training needs," the deceptive in-service "training needs assessment," or "facilities needs," doing so confuses means with ends. For example, if we start identifying "facilities needs," when we are anxious to get long lead time items, such as buildings, funded and constructed, we should first identify the needs to which they would be responsive. How embarrassing and wasteful to build a new school only to realize before it is open that it was too small and/or it would not accommodate the curriculum and methods of tomorrow.

A *quasi need* is a gap between what is and what should be for inputs and/or processes. It only makes sense to deal with a quasi need after we have identified and selected the needs that it will meet. To do otherwise places us in the position of selecting means that might not deliver useful ends. Because of the wide-spread ends/means confusion, most so-called needs assessments are actually quasi needs assessments.

3.7 Needs Assessments Will Find Problems, Identify What Shouldn't Be Changed, and Recognize Opportunities

A. *Yes, and . . .*

In our world of media coverage, it is catchy to criticize all of education and state that everything must be thrown out and we should start over. That's nonsense—attention grabbing—but nonsense. Although there is much to change, we should be careful also (a) to maintain what is working and (b) to identify future opportunities and directions.

Although most current attention in education is related to reactive actions for fixing, repairing, modifying, and responding to crises, we also have other concerns.

B. *Resolving Problems Using Needs Assessment*

Reactive responses to problems are vital when things are going wrong; we have to stop the hemorrhaging before changing the diet. Most educational organizations have plenty of problems that demand immediate attention: low student achievement, vandalism, improperly certified teachers filling vacant slots, drug use in school and on the streets. Where there are problems, both surfaced and hidden, a needs assessment is important to identify the gaps in results, place them in priority order, and select the most important for resolution. Needs selected for reduction or elimination are defined as "problems."

C. *Maintaining What's Working*

Not everything has to be changed. Remember that there are many things going on in education that should be maintained.

Much of education should be preserved by design, not modified while sweeping changes are being made to resolve other problems. Rather than changing what's working, we best continuously improve the areas where there are no gaps in performance (needs). These areas should be flagged to

    (a) make certain that no changes are made to successful means and resources and/or

    (b) develop methods and means to continue to improve what's working so that needs will not emerge.

In-service training experiences, for example, might be selected on the basis of maintaining and reinforcing teacher abilities. By maintaining their competence, learner performance will not decline below expected levels: Learner performance-related needs will not emerge. If student achievement is already at required levels, do not shift what is being done (from differentiated staffing to open classrooms, or from computer-aided instruction to peer tutoring) unless performance will be improved even more. Also, another possibility for maintenance could be computer-aided record keeping to assure that teacher time is not switched from learning management to bookkeeping—again, to maintain learner performance levels.

Another dimension for maintenance is in the area of continuous improvement of abilities and resources so that needs do not appear. For example, if learners are performing to expectations in a subject matter area, teachers might benefit from in-service training in new developments in the field so that the competencies of students will be aligned with later schooling and societal requirements and realities. Therefore no new needs will develop.

D. *Opportunity Finding*

In addition to identifying needs and associated problems, there is the proactive task of identifying future requirements so that future needs will not develop and/or so that we can identify a new direction in which to steer. This assessment would identify gaps between what is and what could be.

For example, it is clear that the workplace of tomorrow will require substantial information technology abilities (Toffler, 1990). In addition, cooperative working will be in greater demand instead of only using the individual performance skills that are the target of most current educational practice. Standard educational practice focuses on individual performance, from testing to recitation to work projects and reports. Most jobs and interpersonal successes require that group learning and responses be made. If we only transfer individual, private abilities to our learners, where do the cooperative ones come from? Rather than waiting for performance deficits to appear in tomorrow's world (loss in the standard of living through low productivity, continued disintegration of the family and personal relationships, crime, aggression, and so on), an assessment would seek to identify future requirements and use those in planning educational responses.

E. *An Integrated Approach: NOM Assessment*

Because it is vital to identify *needs, opportunities,* and *maintenance* requirements, all three perspectives are worth including as part of strategic thinking and planning: a *NOM assessment.* The basic concepts underlying needs assessments still hold: The nuclei are still results and priorities. A possible format for a NOM assessment, building on the elements of needs assessments, is shown in Table 3.5.

3.8 Objectives, Needs Assessment, and the Seven Basic Questions

Table 1.2 provided seven basic questions that every organization has to ask and answer. The first three questions address ends, and thus objectives for those levels can and should be prepared. Questions 4 and 5 address means, and thus objectives for them are best labeled "quasi objectives" to show that we might want to target them but only after relating each to a result.

TABLE 3.5 NOM Assessment Table

Current Results	Desired Results	Need Exists?		Maintenance Required?		Future Opportunities
		Yes	No	Yes	No	

NOTE: In this format for a NOM assessment, needs, opportunities, and maintenance factors are included.

For each of the first three questions, not only will objectives be written but each can serve as the basis for a statement of need, as shown in Table 3.6. Question 1 also opens the door to identifying future opportunities for the educational system, identifying new objectives and directions. Question 3 also addresses maintaining what is working.

The needs-based objectives that were the answers to Questions 1, 2, and 3 serve as the basis for answering Questions 4 and 5, which concern (a) means that are based upon the ends to be accomplished and (b) closing the gaps that are confirmed by the needs assessment.

Evaluation, or Questions 6 and 7, may be based upon the same criteria as those used in the objectives (Questions 1, 2, and 3). These same criteria also provide the "what should be" dimensions of the need statement.

There is a tight relationship among the three levels of results, the nature and structure of objectives, and the needs statements, as shown in Figure 3.3.

Because of these interconnections, strategic thinking, planning, objectives, needs assessment, management, and evaluation are all integrated and related.

TABLE 3.6 The Gaps in Results for the Five Basic Organizational Questions Posed in Needs Assessment Terms

TYPE OF NEEDS ASSESSMENT AND QUASI NEEDS ASSESSMENT FOCUS		QUESTIONS TO BE ASKED AND ANSWERED
NEEDS: Mega/Outcome	#1	Do you care about the success of learners after they leave your educational system and are citizens?
Macro/Output	#2	Do you care about the quality --competence-- of the completers and leavers when they leave your educational system?
Micro/Product	#3	Do you care about the specific skills, knowledges, attitudes, and abilities of the learners as they move from course to course, and level to level?
QUASI NEEDS: Process	#4	Do you care about the efficiency of your educational programs, activities, and methods?
Input	#5	Do you care about the quality and availability of your educational resources, including human, capital, financial, and learning?

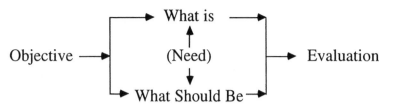

Figure 3.3. The Relationships Among Objectives, Needs, and Evaluation

3.9 Restructuring That Will Really Change the System for the Better

Rather than nibbling around the edges of educational restructuring (shifting schedules, adding courses, using educational technology), restructuring or reengineering can be justified and made demonstrably effective by using the strategic planning framework (Chapter 2) and designing the changes with the basic concepts and tools provided here.

Earlier, we noted that well-intentioned educational change has rarely caused systemic and continuous improvement. Good ideas have failed for the wrong reasons simply because the selection of means was not related to a mega-level vision and mission. It is quite likely that many of the not so successful changes we have attempted in the past will make an excellent contribution when they are linked to objectives and needs firmly anchored in societal results and payoffs.

3.10 The Basic Steps of Educational System Planning

We have identified six Critical Success Factors, a framework for strategic planning and thinking, and the basic building blocks of objectives and needs assessment. In the following chapters, you will be provided the steps and specifics on doing useful planning. There is one more concept, or tool, that will be useful any time you want to get from your current results to

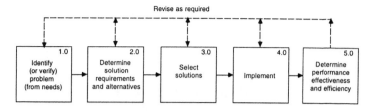

Figure 3.4. A General Problem-Solving Process
SOURCE: Based on Kaufman (1988b); used with permission.
NOTE: The last step (revise as required) is indicated by the broken lines and may take place during any problem-solving step.

desired ones: a six-step problem identification and resolution model (Kaufman, 1972, 1992b). The six steps are shown in Figure 3.4.

Step 1 deals with needs—gaps in results—and selects those for reduction or elimination. When a need is selected for resolution or reduction, it is called a "problem": no gap in results, no need; no need, no problem. Critical Success Factors 2, 3, 4, 5, and 6 come into play here.

Step 2 derives detailed objectives and for each one identifies (but does not select) possible ways and means for meeting them. Critical Success Factors 3 and 5 and the ABCD format are important here. At this step, detailed objectives for resolving the problem selected in Step 1 are prepared, and possible methods and means are identified *but* not selected—we simply seek to determine whether there is at least one way to meet the objectives. Selection takes place in the next step.

In Step 3, the methods and means are selected for each objective or family of related objectives. The selection is based on the cost and consequences for each alternative "how" identified in Step 2.

Step 4 is the management, implementation, and control of resolving the problems and meeting the objectives.

Step 5 is summative evaluation. Based on the criteria in the objectives (from 1 and 2), results are compared with intentions. Decisions are made on what to change and what to continue.

Step 6 is really continuous evaluation and revision while planning and then later in implementation. The purpose of this step is to revise as required along the way to resolving the problems. Rather than waiting until Step 5 to revise, midcourse corrections and changes are to be made to best assure that the needs will be met and the problem resolved.

Steps 5 and 6 deal with evaluation: finding out where planning and implementation have failed and where they are working. It is crucial to keep in mind that evaluation data should be used to fix—continuously improve—not blame.

These six problem-solving steps, shown as a flowchart (or management plan) in Figure 3.3, may be used each time you want to define and then get from what is to what should be.

3.11 Strategic Planning: Reviewing the Six Critical Success Factors

Most tasks require the right tools and the right blueprint. Educational planning is no exception. Mega-level planning depends upon using the Critical Success Factors—the basis for what is in our tool chest, as shown in Table 3.7.

The themes of the six Critical Success Factors will reappear throughout this book. And maybe that *is* simple, straightforward, and correct.

Let's not oversimplify or make things more complex than they are. We can, simply and practically, define where we are going, justify why we should be going there, and then use the six Critical Success Factors.

Key Terms

❑ *Objective.* A statement of intended results that includes (a) what results are to be obtained, (b) who or what will display the result, (c) under what conditions the result will be observed, and (d) what criteria (using interval or ratio scale measurement) will be used.

❑ *Mission objective.* A mission statement plus measurable criteria.

TABLE 3.7 The Six Critical Success Factors for Thinking and
Planning Strategically

CRITICAL SUCCESS FACTOR #1:	MOVE OUT OF TODAY'S COMFORT ZONES AND USE NEW AND WIDER BOUNDARIES FOR THINKING, PLANNING, DOING, AND EVALUATING.
CRITICAL SUCCESS FACTOR #2:	DIFFERENTIATE BETWEEN ENDS AND MEANS (focus on what not how).
CRITICAL SUCCESS FACTOR #3:	USE ALL THREE LEVELS OF RESULTS (Mega, Macro, and Micro).
CRITICAL SUCCESS FACTOR #4.	USE AN IDEAL VISION AS THE UNDERLYING BASIS FOR PLANNING (don't be limited to your organization)
CRITICAL SUCCESS FACTOR #5.	PREPARE OBJECTIVES--INCLUDING MISSION OBJECTIVES--WHICH INCLUDE MEASURES OF HOW YOU WILL KNOW WHEN YOU HAVE ARRIVED (Mission statement plus success criteria).
CRITICAL SUCCESS FACTOR #6.	DEFINE "NEED" AS A GAP IN RESULTS (not as insufficient levels of resources, means, or methods)

❑ *Need.* The gap between current results and desired/required ones.
❑ *Needs assessment.* The process that
  • identifies gaps between current results and desired ones,
  • prioritizes the gaps in results (needs), and
  • selects the most important needs for closure or reduction.
❑ *Soft data.* Data based upon individual perceptions that are not independently verifiable.
❑ *Hard data.* Data based on independently verifiable performance.
❑ *Value added.* The extent to which we recover costs and deliver beyond the break-even point for a delivered output, or result.

❑ *Quasi need / quasi needs assessment.* A gap in processes or resources (but not a gap in results) or the collection and prioritizing of gaps in processes or resources; sometimes confused with needs assessment, which causes means, methods, and/or resources to be selected without linking them to gaps in performance.

❑ *Organizational elements model (OEM).* The elements, and their relationships, that describe what organizations use, do, accomplish, deliver as well as their impact outside of themselves. The organizational elements are

inputs: the ingredients, or starting conditions, used by the organization;

processes: the methods, means, activities, programs, and "how-to's" used to turn the inputs into accomplishments;

products: the building-block results accomplished by working with the inputs and using the processes (micro-level results);

outputs: the results that are or could be delivered to society (macro-level results);

outcomes: the external—outside the school or system—payoffs and consequences of the inputs, processes, products, and outputs in and for the society and community (mega-level results).

❑ *NOM assessment.* The identification of *needs, opportunities,* and *maintenance* requirements. This is important so that (a) needs are identified, (b) opportunities are sought (and not only in a reactive problem-solving mode), and (c) you maintain that which is currently successful.

❑ *Problem identification and resolution model (six steps).* A framework and steps for (a) identifying problems (based on needs); (b) determining detailed performance requirements and identifying possible methods and means for meeting the requirements; (c) selection of methods and means; (d) implementation; (e) determining effectiveness and efficiency of performance; and an ongoing step, (f) revising as required.

Note

1. The use of the mnemonic *ABCD* is not original, but variations define the elements somewhat differently.

4

Mega-Level Planning:
The Larger Community and Society

The three phases of strategic planning are

- Scoping
- Planning
- Implementation and evaluation/continuous improvement

Regardless of the selected scope—mega, macro, or micro—the steps for being strategic are the same (see, e.g., Kaufman, 1988, 1992b; Kaufman, Herman, & Watters, in press). This chapter provides the elements of mega-level planning. The two chapters that follow (Chapters 5 and 6) deal with the particulars of macro- and micro-level planning.

4.1 Scoping

When your primary concern is for today's and tomorrow's world, select the mega level. At this level, the primary client and beneficiary of what gets planned and delivered is today's and tomorrow's society and world. This is the most practical choice of all.

Obtain agreement on the mega level of strategic planning. It is vital that the planning partners first agree on the mega level of planning. This chapter assumes that the mega level has been selected. If everyone has made the selection, move ahead. If another level is chosen by the planning partners, then go to Chapter 5 for macro-level planning or to Chapter 6 for micro-level planning. In case the planning partners are open to reconsidering their premature jump to macro or micro planning, then review with them the advantages of mega planning first. Use the relationships among the level selected and subsequent activities and results (Figure 4.1).

To assure that all educational partners understand that the entire system intends to work at the mega level and contribute to an ideal vision, employing an agreement table (see Table 4.1) may be helpful. Ask all partners (internal and external) formally to accept or reject each proposition. Notice that, if a planning partner or stakeholder rejects any proposition, he or she becomes responsible for its nonachievement.

4.2 Mega Level Is the Ideal Vision

A. *Mega-Level Planning and "Front-End Alignment"*

Each person in an educational organization and everything he or she does and produces are linked. A way to view mega-level planning is to note that the frames, or layers, of educational planning, doing, delivery, and consequences are aligned or nested and contribute to each other. Figure 4.2 demonstrates the importance of alignment in what is done, used, and accomplished. What would happen if only one of the arrow heads were to disappear? Integration and alignment, from the front end and

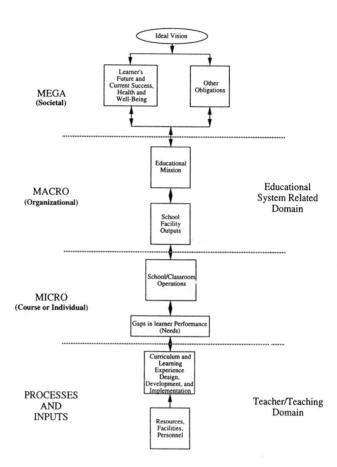

Figure 4.1. Aligning Needs Identification With the Ideal Vision

throughout, are vital. Any needs assessment and subsequent actions should be part of this alignment, as shown in Figure 4.2.

B. Derive the Ideal Vision

After selecting the mega level, derive an ideal vision: Define the world in which we want tomorrow's child to live. Although

TABLE 4.1 Educational Strategic Planning Agreement Table

		Response			
		Stake-holders		Planners	
		Y	N	Y	N
1.	Each school, as well as the total educational system, should contribute to the learners' current and future success survival, health, and well-being.				
2.	Each school, as well as the total educational system, should contribute to the learners' current and future quality of life.				
3.	Learners' current and future survival, health, and well-being will be part of the system's and each of its schools' mission objectives.				
4.	Each educational function will have objectives that contribute to 1, 2, and 3.				
5.	Each job/task/activity will have objectives that contribute to 1, 2, 3, and 4.				
6.	A needs assessment will identify and document any gaps in results at the operational levels of 1, 2, 3, 4, and 5.				
7.	Educational learning requirements will be generated from the needs identified and selected based on the results of 6.				
8.	The results of 6 may recommend noneducational intervention.				
9.	Evaluation will use data from comparing results with objectives for 1, 2, 3, 4, and 5.				

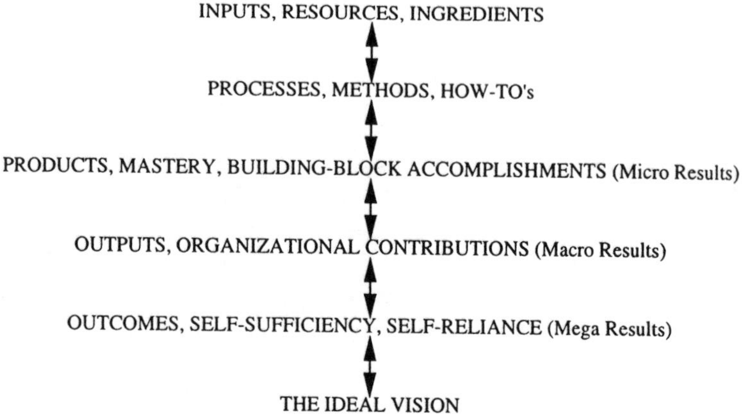

INPUTS, RESOURCES, INGREDIENTS

↕

PROCESSES, METHODS, HOW-TO's

↕

PRODUCTS, MASTERY, BUILDING-BLOCK ACCOMPLISHMENTS (Micro Results)

↕

OUTPUTS, ORGANIZATIONAL CONTRIBUTIONS (Macro Results)

↕

OUTCOMES, SELF-SUFFICIENCY, SELF-RELIANCE (Mega Results)

↕

THE IDEAL VISION

Figure 4.2. An Educational System Results Chain
NOTE: Every element must be directly linked with each other element
for the system to work.

it is conventional strategic planning practice to define beliefs
and values first, it is not a productive approach. Doing so allows
the strongly held "philosophies" and ways of viewing the world
to drive and bias the future view rather than allowing our vision
to drive what we do and accomplish today and tomorrow. Many
accepted approaches do start with defining beliefs and values
(e.g., Cook, 1990). Starting there assumes that the educational
partner's beliefs and values are immutable and unchangeable.
Worse, starting with existing beliefs and values assumes that
they are all correct and useful. Recall the many positive changes
we have had recently related to previously strongly held beliefs
and values concerning ageism, sexism, racism.

First, define the world for tomorrow's child, which will allow
people to examine their beliefs and values. Review the rationale
provided in Chapter 2, especially in Figure 2.3. Table 4.2 provides a sample format for obtaining planning partner perceptions of an "ideal vision" or preferred future. The format breaks
the task into two stages: first, a statement (excluding means
and resources) of the ideal and, then, an identification of criteria
that could be used to measure success or progress.

TABLE 4.2 A Possible Format for Obtaining Partner Perceptions of an Ideal Vision/Preferred Future

Ideal Vision/Preferred Future
Describe the world in which you want tomorrow's child to live:

ENDS/Results Criteria
(e.g., 0 deaths or disabilities from illicit drugs; no murders; no rapes; no species become extinct from human intervention.)

Practical dreaming. In its most powerful use, strategic planning identifies results based upon an ideal vision: a mega-level dream. To be useful, an ideal vision has to

(a) be future oriented and unfettered by any constrained or negative thinking, which are often seen in education; it is an ideal and as such defines the kind of world we want for our children and grandchildren;

(b) identify a clear set of conditions, written in a format using all the ABCD elements (see Table 3.1) for objectives;

(c) be devoid of means, methods, and "how-to's" and, instead, focus on tangible results;

(d) project hope, energy, destination, not despair, distrust, or negative competition.

This vision should not be centered on rivalry (e.g., better test results than Japan or fewer dropouts than Watters County), rather, it motivates and encourages everyone to enlist in the adventure. Walt Disney was right, if we can dream it, we can do it.

From this ideal, we set stepping-stone strategic objectives that will get us from our current results ever closer to the ideal (Figure 2.3).

Continuous improvement as we move toward the ideal vision. The achievement of the stepping-stone results will take time: Micro results might start to appear this year; macro results, within the next 2 to 3 years; mega results, in 3 to 10 years; and the ideal vision, 40 years or more in the future. For example, if part of our preferred future includes everyone being able to get and keep a job above the poverty level in Grise Township, our schools might achieve that by the year 2000; graduates and completers will have the requisite skills, knowledge, attitudes, and abilities by 1998; and the building-block competencies will start to be demonstrated by learners starting next year. The ideal vision from which this all flowed might have been this: "Every graduate or completer from the Greater Grise Township schools will be self-sufficient and self-reliant and not under the care, custody, or control of another person, agency, or substance."

The nature of ideal visions: More similar than different. An ideal vision speaks to a perfect future. Regardless of the nature of the organization (a steel company, a school, a governmental health agency, or the army), ideal visions will be quite similar. Because all organizations, educational ones included, are means to societal ends, their societal visions will be similar. When getting your planning partners to think about the world they want for their children and grandchildren, a very appealing place gets defined.

For example, here is an ideal vision developed by one public sector health and human services organization:

Our citizens have a bright future. People take charge of their lives, become healthy and self-sufficient. Families are strong, self-reliant, and productive. Neighborhoods are safe, supportive, and prosperous and residents contribute their best abilities to their community. This vision will become real as we trust people, as we earn the public's trust through our own excellence, and as we are full partners with people, families, and neighborhoods.

Compare that ideal vision with this one for a mining company:

The world will be safe for every living thing. There will be no species which become endangered or extinct. There will be no murder, rape, war, or psychological or physical abuse. People will acquire the skills and abilities to be self-sufficient and self-reliant and will assist others to acquire those same skills and values so that less than 1% of the population will ever be temporarily (less than 6 months) requiring social welfare. Water will be available and clean, so that no one will get ill or die from contamination. No one will die from starvation, thirst, contamination in their homes, lands, food, water, or air.

Here is an educational organization's ideal vision:

The world will be at peace, and there will be no murders, rapes, or crimes, nor substance abuse. It will be free of debilitating infectious disease, and every child brought into the world will be a wanted child. Poverty will not exist, and every woman and man will earn as much as it costs them to live unless they are going to school and moving toward preparing themselves to be self-sufficient and self-reliant. The unlucky and unfortunate among us will be helped to help themselves so that they are increasingly close to being self-sufficient and self-reliant. People will take charge of their lives and be responsible for what they use, do, and contribute. Personal, intimate, and loving partnerships will form and sustain themselves. Government's primary contribution will be assisting people to be happy and self-sustaining, and will reinforce independence and mutual contribution and will be organized and funded to the extent to which it meets its objectives. U.S. business will earn a profit without bringing harm to its clients and our mutual world.

These ideal visions possess three of the four elements discussed in preparing useful visions. They each lack the measurable criteria necessary to gauge success.

Adding measurable criteria. Each ideal vision should include measurable criteria so that anything derived from it can be calibrated and the partners can measure the organization's success. Here are some criteria for the above educational organization ideal vision:

The world will be at peace (as certified by the United Nations), and there will be no murders, rapes, crimes, or substance abuse (as certified by the U.S. Department of Justice). It will be free of debilitating infectious disease (as certified by the Centers for Disease Control), and every child brought into the world will be a wanted child (as indicated by no child living below the poverty level, zero child abuse convictions, and so on). Poverty will not exist, and every woman and man will earn as much as it costs them to live unless they are going to school and moving toward preparing themselves to be self-sufficient and self-reliant (as certified by the U.S. Department of Labor). The unlucky and unfortunate among us will be helped to help themselves so that they are increasingly close to being self-sufficient and self-reliant (as indicated by an increase in life expectancies for this population and increase in the amount of money their work produces and contributes to their subsistence, and so on). People will take charge of their lives, and be responsible for what they use, do, and contribute (as indicated by no incarcerations, no personal abuse of others, and the like). Personal, intimate, and loving partnerships will form and sustain themselves (as indicated by a zero divorce rate, no judgments of physical abuse for persons living together, and so on). Government's primary contribution will be assisting people to be happy and self-sustaining and will reinforce independence and mutual contribution and will be organized and funded to the extent to which it meets its objectives (as indicated by funding levels and mega results referenced by agency budgets and evaluations). U.S. business will earn a profit without bringing harm to its clients and our mutual world (as reported by the U.S. Departments of Commerce, the Interior, and Health & Human Services).

C. Relating the Mega-Level Vision

Before going further, let's relate an ideal vision in order to link to the mission. When preparing a mission objective, there is a rolling down from the ideal vision to identify exactly what your organization can and will contribute to it. If any organization cannot connect its current or future contributions to a preferred future, it is on its way to extinction: It is a solution to no known problem!

Figure 2.4 (in Chapter 2) shows how the mega-level-linked mission objective only takes on parts of the ideal vision. The educational (Macro-level) mission, and thus everything that follows, rolls down from the ideal vision and takes on only those parts to which it will contribute.

In relating mega, macro, and micro levels of planning, visualize connected frames within frames (Figure 4.3). Seen in this way, the external world (and its survival and quality) is a driver for what education targets, and this in turn drives what the educational system delivers, accomplishes, does, and uses. Evaluation determines the extent to which the results at the various levels are mutually contributing.

Mega-level planning will use all of the frames in thinking and planning. (This same framework will appear in the next two chapters with the lower levels of contributions emphasized.)

But not everyone is comfortable with setting ideal visions, even though they have selected the mega level. Following are some considerations in working with those who get nervous about developing an ideal vision.

(1) Special patience with process-oriented people is necessary. (The HRD/training director of a large medical facility notes that some people are "PPPs": purely process persons.) Their unique skills and contributions will be vital when agreement is reached on directions and resources can be justified. The only differences will be that more resources will be justifiable and

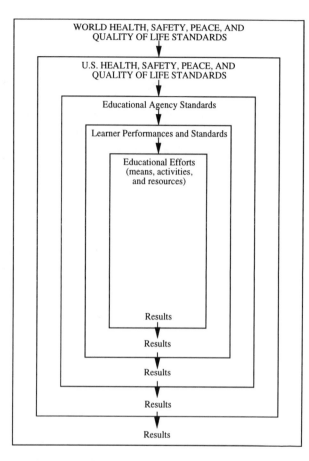

Figure 4.3. Nested Frames Within Which Educational Results and Processes Relate to the External World in Which They All Operate and Must Contribute

thus available. These helping/assisting people will, along with everyone else, contribute to the common good and ideal destiny.

(2) Pay gentle attention to the planning partners. Get them to think in terms of (a) results, (b) defining and using an ideal vision that is tangible and measurable, and/or (c) encouraging some partners to understand that they are being asked to operate outside of their usual comfort zones and that they con-

sider the possibilities of change as having more rewards than returning to more comfortable (and less functional) ideas.

(3) Assurances should be provided that a favorite means (computers, values education, and so on) will not be lost or be forgotten. Set up an "Important Ideas" list and, as a planning partner suggests a means, write it, very publicly, on that list. Promise to revisit the list when methods and means are later identified and selected—and keep your promise.

Useful, justifiable, proactive strategic thinking and planning depends upon an ideal vision. Remember Critical Success Factor 4: Use an ideal vision as the underlying basis for planning (don't be limited by current restraints or by nay-sayers). Going directly to macro- or micro-level planning should not be given in to easily.

D. *Identify Current Mission(s) and Translate Into Mission Objectives*

It is unusual for a school or district not to have a mission statement. The advantage of having one is that they are already thinking about the future and their destinations. The disadvantages of having a mission statement come from the following: (a) Most have been derived with a lot of effort, and people are heavily invested in them; (b) they usually are missing measurable criteria for results; (c) most deal with means and not ends; and therefore (d) they are mission statements, not mission objectives, and usually have little to do the with mega-level expectations.

Transform the existing mission statement into mission objectives by adding measurable (interval and/or ratio scale) criteria. Recall Critical Success Factor 5: Prepare objectives—including mission objectives—that include measures of how you will know when you have arrived. At the mega level, the mission objective will include measurable criteria that deal directly with societal payoffs and consequences:

mission statement + measurable criteria = mission objective

TABLE 4.3 A Format and Procedure for Assuring That Your
Mission Is Useful, Deals With Ends and Not Means,
and Has Mega-Level Expectations

Mission Elements:	Target		Ends Level		
	Means	Ends	Micro	Macro	Mega
a)					
b)					
c)					
etc...					

NOTE: Step 1: List each element of the mission. Step 2: For each, determine if it relates to a means or an end. Step 3: If an element relates
to an end, determine whether it is focused at the micro, macro, or mega
level. Step 4: If an element relates to a means, ask: "What result would
I get if I got or accomplished this?" Keep asking the same question until
an end is identified.

Table 4.3 provides a format and procedure for translating mission statements into mission objectives at the mega level and
for assuring that you have all three levels of results covered and
related.

This process is useful for any derivation of objectives,
whether at the mega, macro, or micro levels. It is essential, in
keeping with Critical Success Factors 2 and 3, to assure that
objectives deal with ends and that all three levels of ends are
considered and linked.

E. Relate and Align Beliefs and Values

Beliefs and values are perceptions, usually unexamined and
strongly held. They represent the planning partners' current realities. Beliefs and values usually focus on means, resources,
and "how-to's." They often have such names as "my educational
philosophy" or "my view of education."

Beliefs and values may or may not be supported by facts and
research, but they are important to each educational partner.

TABLE 4.4 A Process for Aligning Beliefs and Values with the
Ideal Vision

Beliefs and values are best considered when deriving the ideal vision
and not as a separate step or exercise. If beliefs and values come up
during later phases of planning, the following steps will assist you
in aligning them with the ideal vision. Rather than independently
collecting beliefs and values and risking that they will be accepted
without questioning their usefulness in terms of getting continuously closer to the ideal vision, the following are suggested:

1. Define the ideal vision in measurable terms. All of the elements
    should deal with ends and none with means or resources. All
    elements should describe the world desired for tomorrow's child.

2. List each of the elements of the ideal vision, and check to assure
    that each element
    a. targets an end (no means or resources are included), and
    b. is at the mega/societal level.

3. If any element is not an end at the mega/societal level, ask "if
    this were accomplished, what societal result and payoff would it
    deliver?" Keep asking this question until the societal/mega end
    is identified and substitute it for the lower-level end or means
    earlier identified.

4. List any beliefs and values which have surfaced (e.g., outcome-
    based education should be used, increase student hours, parents
    must be actively involved).

5. Ask, for each belief and value, "if this was true and/or implemented
    as part of our educational enterprise, what would be the societal
    results and payoffs delivered?"

6. If a belief and value results in mega level results, it is probably
    useful and should be considered when selecting methods and
    means. If it will not demonstrably lead to a mega/societal result,
    do not use it.

When you start dredging them up, emotional responses are sure
to follow. Keep away from value judgments and allow the responses to surface publicly. Table 4.4 provides a format for linking beliefs and values to an ideal vision.

Ask the partners to use the ideal vision they have developed in rethinking their beliefs and values. By doing so, some self-examination and critical thinking should emerge. Allow for enlightened shifts, modifications, and growth.

An open and objective discussion concerning beliefs and values is sometimes useful when necessary. With each person hearing the positions of the others, common bonds and directions can be formed. In guiding the mutual exploration of beliefs and values, an ends/means analysis may be helpful:

1. Collect individual statements of beliefs and values.
2. Extract common and unique beliefs and values.
3. Present the common and unique beliefs and values to the group and ask them to sort each into ends and means.
4. Ask the group to identify those that will contribute to the ideal vision and those that will not.
5. Construct a list of agreed-upon beliefs and values.

F. Identify Needs

Problems are needs selected for resolution. At the mega level of thinking and planning, the ideal vision is compared with existing conditions/results, and the gaps are the needs.

Figure 4.4 shows the relationship between an ideal vision and current conditions/results that both form the basis for the identification of mega-level needs and provide the basis for further planning and accomplishment.

After the gaps in results are identified, a needs assessment summary may be constructed. A format for the needs assessment summary is provided in Table 3.4 in Chapter 3. Notice again in that table that the first column lists current results; the second, possible methods and means for closing the gaps; and the third identifies required results. Not ignoring the inevitable methods and means (e.g., computer-aided instruction, higher teacher salaries, open enrollment), but placing them on the form to languish until each can be linked to a need, dignifies the contributions of planning partners. At the same time, it reminds everyone that solutions should be selected only after the needs have been identified and prioritized and the problems selected.

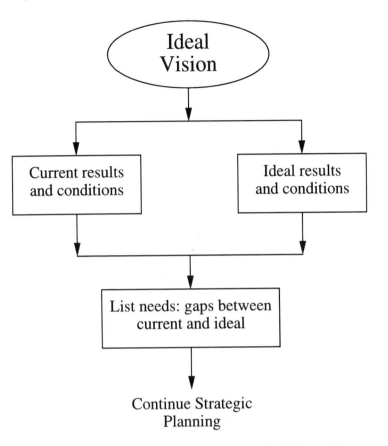

Figure 4.4. The Relationship Between an Ideal Vision, Current Conditions and Results, and Further Planning

A needs assessment checklist is provided in Table 4.5. After doing a needs assessment, or while work is being done, check off the items.

A NOM (needs, opportunities, maintenance) assessment also may be done at this juncture. For each "what is" and "what should be," identify those needs that should be closed, those critical areas for which there are no gaps *and* there shouldn't be, and areas where there will be gaps in the future if you don't attend to them soon. Also, based upon the ideal vision, identify those areas for which new objectives (even at the mission level) might be considered. A NOM format is provided in Table 3.5 in Chapter 3.

TABLE 4.5 A Checklist for Selecting or Designing a Needs
Assessment

---

1. Does it target ends rather than means?

2. Does it cover the three levels or organizational concerns:
    - Micro (or products);
    - Macro (or outputs);
    - Mega (or outcomes)?

3. Is it free from assumptions concerning the solution (such as training, human resources development, total quality management, "excellence")?

4. Does it collect and use perception data about gaps in results from each of the three partner groups (recipients, implementers, and society/community)?

5. Does it collect and use performance-based results and not just the perceptions of the partners?

6. Does it identify the gaps in results in measurable performance terms?

7. Does it integrate the perception data with the performance data?

8. Does it place the gaps in priority order?

G. Identify Matches and Mismatches, Agreements and Disagreements

There are now hard data (from the needs assessment) and soft data (from the ideal vision and the beliefs and values). The next vital task is to compare these and identify where the hard data and the soft data agree and disagree.

Figure 4.5 shows the framework for merging hard and soft data to assure that objectives are valid, useful, and acceptable. It also shows the areas for collecting more data.

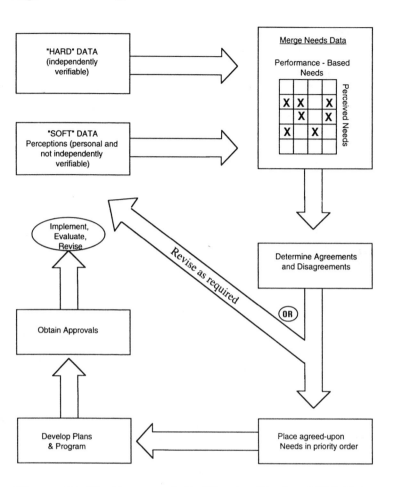

Figure 4.5. The Framework for Merging Hard and Soft Data
SOURCE: Based on Kaufman (1988b); used with permission.

It is important that agreement exists among the sources of data. Otherwise, the partners, and the interests they represent, won't perceive the needs assessment data base as useful and they won't accept the results. Where there isn't accord, initiate further fact finding or reeducate the needs assessment and planning partners so they can agree.

H. *Obtain Agreement: Reconcile Differences*

Before setting priorities, deriving objectives, and selecting interventions, which is the balance of strategic planning, the partners must agree on a set of needs. They must assure that the objectives based on the hard and soft data agree, are coherent, and will contribute to the achievement of the ideal vision. When there are disagreements, help the partners come to agreement. Tools for obtaining agreement are (a) technical and (b) group-process oriented.

Technical resolution possibilities include the following:

Reconcile the perceived (soft data) needs with those based on actual performance (hard data).

Derive a common set of needs supported by both the hard and the soft data and request additional data if there are insurmountable differences.

Translate the disputed perceived needs into results. Ask the partners if the revision represents their concern. If it doesn't, ask them to revise it into a results-oriented statement that will address the concern. Most arguments over needs come from an incorrect (and usually tenacious) adherence to talking about gaps in methods and resources (quasi needs) rather than actual gaps in results.

Ask the disagreeing partners to define the result that will be obtained if a certain "need" were met. This encourages the partners to track the linkages from inputs and processes to results and then to a defined gap in results. Then they can sensibly rank the needs—now gaps in results—for resolution.

Sometimes there are differences that seem to stall everything. Don't go ahead without basic agreement, and don't capitulate just to keep the peace. Most partners are honorable, concerned, and want to identify and meet the right needs. Often what is missing are additional data.

Group-process oriented resolution possibilities include the following:

Discourage special interest groups. These groups should not push a pet solution—such as computer-aided instruction or quality management training—a method—such as self-paced or multimedia instruction—or a resource—such as money or people—without first identifying and selecting which need their favorite solution is intended to address.

Encourage and model the behavior yourself for all partners to define needs as gaps in results.

Be patient and open. Allow people to express their fears (they will use another label) because they have been pushed outside of their comfort zone. Listen.

When disagreement still lingers, you often will have to revisit the historical context and the futures data to provide a frame of reference concerning "what was," "what is," "what will be," and "what could be" and finally selecting "what should be." Again, most disagreements stem from (a) confusing ends and means, (b) insisting on a favored means and not being open to first defining gaps in results (needs) before finding an appropriate means, (c) some people operating outside of their usual comfort zones and externalizing blame rather than looking inside themselves to consider more useful but initially less familiar alternatives, and/or (d) people playing power games. Bring these possibilities up with the planning partners and list the existing "needs." Make up a simple chart with the "needs" in a first column, and two other columns marked "ends" and "means." Have the group fill out the chart; they will usually notice that some premature "means" have slipped in and will eliminate them.

I. Select Long- and Short-Term Missions

Keeping in mind the characteristics of objectives, identify the missions for the future (which rolls down from the ideal vision, as shown in Figure 2.3).

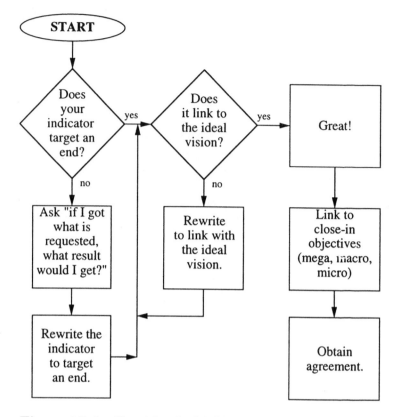

Figure 4.6. An Algorithm for Linking Indicators to an Ideal Vision to Help Achieve a Useful and Common Set of Results

Each of these mission objectives should (a) be based upon the now-shared ideal vision, needs, and mission and (b) precisely identify where the educational organization is headed, and how everyone will know when (and if) they have arrived. Because measurable criteria are used, progress toward each of the missions and the ideal may be plotted and reported. Appropriate responses, resources, and en route changes may be related.

When developing mission objectives, check to assure that each one will make a contribution to the ideal vision. Figure 4.6 supplies an algorithm for assuring the linkages between objectives and the chain of results from micro to macro to mega (the ideal vision).

4.3 Planning

A. *Identify Strengths, Weaknesses, Opportunities, and Threats*

Every educational agency has many things going for it. There are also many things that can or could get in the way of success (Kaufman, Herman, & Watters, in press). Based on where your system is going, and the needs and their priorities, now is the time to identify objectively the system's strengths, weaknesses, opportunities, and threats (SWOTs).

Strengths might include an outstanding local science corporation that is willing to provide talent and resources. A weakness might be a political system that fights over higher versus lower taxes without first agreeing on citizen survival and quality of life levels. Opportunities could include a new no-pollution industry that is moving into the district. Threats might include a new tax shortfall for your state that threatens special education.

The SWOTs will help guide your decisions while moving ever closer to the ideal vision and accomplishing each of the close-in and distant mission objectives.

B. *Derive Decision Rules (Policies)*

There are two uses of *policy*. One, which doesn't seem to be very useful, refers to means and resources—compliance and procedures. The other use, which is preferred for strategic thinking, relates decisions to the shared results. Every person in your organization will have to make decisions. With policies related to ends, not means, useful decisions will be made at all levels, from school discipline to board expenditures.

Policies should be public and available to all. They should be stated in simple, clear terms and avoid "legalese." When policies are no longer useful, modify them.

C. *Develop Strategic Action Plans*

This is the "guts" of being strategic. Based upon the ideal vision, the priority needs, the close-in and distant mission objectives, the SWOTs, and policies, the action plan is developed. The plan should include

(a) the ideal vision;

(b) the mission objectives (and don't forget the performance indicator);

(c) the needs to be addressed in each year between now and the most distant mission objective;

(d) the performances that are to be maintained (and improved) and the opportunities that will be pursued;

(e) the possible methods and means ("how-to's") available for each need, as well as for the selected maintenance requirements and opportunities, and the listing of those methods and means that have been selected;

(f) the scheduling of human, capital, and physical resources along with any development that is required;

(g) the budget for each need (or cluster of needs) and the acquisition schedule for each; and

(h) the evaluation criteria for each need (or cluster of needs).

The mega-level strategic plan should not be long or complex. Ten to twenty pages is often as much as is required. A test of a good strategic plan is the extent to which it is pulled out and used when decisions are made. Another test is whether changes are made to the plan when external reality shifts.

Because the strategic plan is based upon an ideal vision (which, due to its far-in-the-future orientation, is not likely to change easily or quickly), a mega-level strategic plan is likely to remain fairly stable.

If the strategic action plan has been carefully crafted, and each of the six Critical Success Factors has been employed, it will be useful and usable. Review the plan and assure that the Critical Success Factors have been applied throughout.

After the partners have selected the problems to be resolved and have obtained the budget, but before work proceeds, make certain they agree with the anticipated final results. If there is agreement, fine. If agreement does not exist, have them recommend modifications and justify revisions.

4.4 Implementation and Evaluation

A. *Put the Strategic Plan to Work*

The plan was developed to be used. Everyone in the organization should have a copy or easy access to one. Each person should know and agree on his or her unique role and responsibilities and should know exactly how and when he or she will interact with others to achieve the mission and move ever closer to the ideal vision.

The organizational culture—the mores and values of everyone regarding other people as well as the external world and clients—should develop and grow. Not everyone has to buy in to the entire plan, but people should not be allowed to destroy or undermine it. Group norms should handle all but the most corrosive, stubborn, and destructive people.

B. *Conduct Formative Evaluation*

Evaluation is for correcting and fixing, not blaming or condemning. We can and should learn from our experiences, and formative and summative evaluation provide those opportunities for continuous improvement.

Formative evaluation measures progress toward the missions (and the ideal vision). This progress should be continuously tracked. When things are progressing, stay the course. When there are deviations outside of the plan, revise as required.

C. *Conduct Summative Evaluation*

The mission objectives (and their embedded performance indicators) provide the criteria for determining major accomplishments. Periodically, such as at the end of each year, and for each major project (literacy education, physical well-being, total quality initiative), comparisons are to be made on the basis of what was accomplished, and what wasn't. Report what has worked and what has not. Recommendations for what to fix, what to keep, and what to stop are to be made.

D. *Revise as Required, and Keep What's Working*

Based upon comparing the results with the intentions, decisions are made on what to continue, what to modify, and what to stop. Not all interventions (methods and means) will be successful. Even popular programs might be disappointing. Change what has to be changed, add what is missing, and drop what isn't working.

Being strategic is not a one-shot deal. Strategic thinking, planning, and doing are ongoing. After applying this four-phase framework, there are two results:

1. a strategic plan that is rational as well as logical, and, more important,
2. strategic thinking: how everyone goes about doing the day-to-day work.

Strategic thinking is vital. Caring enough about others and an improved and ideal world on a continuing basis is key to success. Use of this process greatly improves the chances that an organizational culture will have results that target both long-term and short-term success.

4.5 Relating Several Varieties of Strategic Planning

There are a number of strategic planning approaches. Most are useful. Most are macro level focused, however, and thus start with the assumption that the goals and objectives of education are known and correct. If you are still convinced that the macro level fits your situation, Chapter 5 is your primary resource.

Another popular (mis)use of the term *strategic planning* has a limiting focus on existing services or disciplines ("strategic" planning for media services; "strategic" planning for professional personnel). If you are still only interested in this micro-level planning, Chapter 6 is your basic referent.

Before you settle for a framework that is different than the one recommended here, one simple appeal: Whether realized or not, all seven strategic questions (Table 1.2) do exist regardless of one's hope or assumptions. Select an approach that will ask and answer all of the questions. Although other approaches are superficially simpler and might cause less discussion and questioning, the gains are likely to be quite expensive in terms of the costs of not getting as close to the ideal vision as humanly and ethically possible.

Think carefully before selecting a quicker fix. What does it cost to do it right versus what will it cost not to?

5

Macro-Level Planning:
The District or School

5.1 When the Primary Beneficiary Is the Educational Organization Itself

Many citizens ask about the quality of our schools and educational systems. They assume that a "good education" will deliver successful citizens and a better society. Confident in their presumption, they mull over graduation rates, dropouts, teenage pregnancies, gang violence, merit scholars, honors graduates, college placement rates, drug-related incidents, and so on. Whether it makes complete sense or not, people usually judge their schools by macro-level indicators (with a few micro-level ones thrown in, such as test scores and literacy data).

In response (and often laboring under similar assumptions), educators report their accomplishments and speculate on ways both to do and to look better. Most citizens don't differentiate much between individual schools when they read the statistics— they only look at district-level indicators such as graduation rates and college placements. When citizens hear about abysmal educational problems, they believe their schools are fine and it is other people's schools with the headaches. Much educational attention has been given to the school as the locus of change, but some observers feel that, while change can happen at the school level, it infrequently generalizes to other schools in the system or to the system itself. After all, students from one school often progress or transfer to others.

If that is the way systems conventionally get judged, then reactions occur at the macro level. Most legislation, strategic planning models, and total quality programs are aimed at the system itself. The frames of reference for macro-level planning are shown in Figure 5.1.

A. *The Primary Questions to Be Asked and Answered at the Macro Level*

Table 5.1 highlights the questions that are the concern of macro thinking and planning. Working at this level assumes either that mega-level results will surely follow *or that work at this level actually builds on mega-level data.*

A macro-level agreement table, a series of expectation statements that planning partners can agree (or disagree) on, is shown in Table 5.2. Each stakeholder should know what is involved in working at the macro level and should note either his or her agreement or disagreement. Without agreement at the outset, "surprises" might derail progress and contribution.

B. *Improving the Outputs of the System*

At the macro level of thinking and planning, the focus is on the outputs of the educational system and its schools (see Table 2.1 for the definition of the Organizational Elements Model and

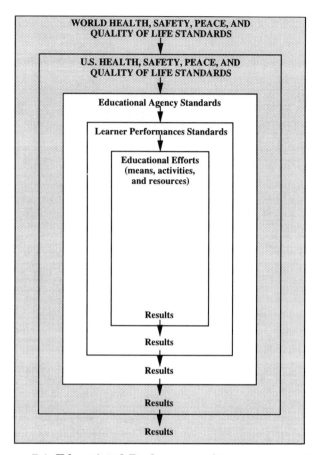

Figure 5.1. Educational Performance, Operations, and Learner Performance as Seen From a Macro-Level Perspective

the five elements, including outputs). The outputs are graduation, completion, and job placement.[1] Macro is the scope of most common strategic planning approaches (see Cook, 1988, 1990; Pfeiffer, Goodstein, & Nolan, 1989) as well as conventional Total Quality Management programs and initiatives. Strategic planning, even at the macro level, can be very effective and efficient.

The improvement of the outputs of an educational system is vital and really beyond reasonable doubt, especially if the macro-level objectives are firmly justified by mega-level data.

TABLE 5.1 Asking the Right Questions: Seven Basic Questions All Educators Should Ask (and answer)

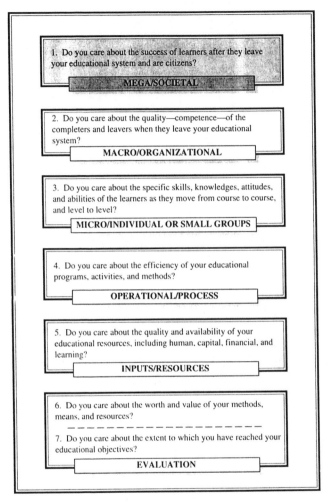

1. Do you care about the success of learners after they leave your educational system and are citizens?

MEGA/SOCIETAL

2. Do you care about the quality—competence—of the completers and leavers when they leave your educational system?

MACRO/ORGANIZATIONAL

3. Do you care about the specific skills, knowledges, attitudes, and abilities of the learners as they move from course to course, and level to level?

MICRO/INDIVIDUAL OR SMALL GROUPS

4. Do you care about the efficiency of your educational programs, activities, and methods?

OPERATIONAL/PROCESS

5. Do you care about the quality and availability of your educational resources, including human, capital, financial, and learning?

INPUTS/RESOURCES

6. Do you care about the worth and value of your methods, means, and resources?

7. Do you care about the extent to which you have reached your educational objectives?

EVALUATION

NOTE: For the macro level, the questions are restricted to 2 through 7.

The definition and extension of an important and useful process for improving the outputs of the system—Total Quality Management—is provided in Chapter 7.

TABLE 5.2 Macro-Level Agreement Table

		Response			
		Stake-holders		Planners	
		Y	N	Y	N
1.	The entire district, including all regular and special schools, will contribute to the graduation, completion, citizenship, and jobs for all learners (adult, special education, vocational, and K-12).				
2.	All curriculum will have measurable objectives that will contribute to 1.				
3.	Each course, activity, and its program elements will contribute to 1 and 2.				
4.	A needs assessment will identify and document gaps between current results and required results at the performance levels for 1, 2, and 3.				
5.	Learning requirements will be generated from the needs identified in 1, 2 and 3 based on the results of 4.				
6.	The results of 4 may recommend activities that are not instructional.				
7.	All activities, materials, methods, and instructional delivery will contribute to 1 and 2.				
8.	Evaluation will use data from comparing results with objectives for 1, 2, 3, and 4, and will identify what is successful and what is to be changed or eliminated.				

The three phases and steps of strategic planning (Figure 2.1) are the same regardless of the scope selected. Following are the steps for being strategic when the macro level has been selected.

5.2 Scoping

At the macro level, the primary client and beneficiary of what gets planned and delivered is the system itself. This has been the conventional choice (and is best when built upon the mega-level ideal vision).

It is essential that the partners agree on the macro level of planning. This chapter assumes that the mega level has been rejected, perhaps only for the moment, or that mega-level planning has already been accomplished. If the micro level is the firm choice of the planning partners, then go to Chapter 6. In case the planning partners are open to reconsidering the premature jump to macro or micro planning, then review with them the advantages of mega planning, which were presented in Chapter 4.

To assure that all educational partners understand that the entire system intends to work at the macro level, employing an agreement table, such as that shown in Table 5.1, may be helpful. Ask each partner (internal and external) formally to accept or reject each proposition. If a planning partner or stakeholder rejects any proposition, he or she assumes responsibility for its nonachievement.

A. *Derive the Educational System (Macro) Objective*[2]

After selecting the macro level, derive a mission for the system and its schools: Define the educational system in which we want to work and what kind of graduates and completers it will provide.

An educational system's mission identifies a clear set of results and conditions for what it is to deliver to society and the community. It defines a destination that allows everyone to contribute to and work toward. It is to be written in the form of any other objective—with the ABCD elements (see Table 3.1 in Chapter 3).

It is essential that the mission be devoid of statements of means, resources, and "how-to's," such as school-based management, more financial resources, more busses, master's-level teachers, a computer in every classroom.

The macro mission should not be competitive with another organization, country, or entity (such as "better test results than Germany," "more merit scholars than Sims County schools," or "win the competitive battle"). Any mission, including a macro one, should identify a set of precise, measurable, rigorously defined results. An educational system mission should project a useful destination, not competition.

An example of an educational system (macro) mission. Here is a hypothetical educational (macro) system mission:

> By the year 2000, all of those who graduate from our system will enroll in accredited higher educational programs or get jobs. All graduates will be good citizens who register to vote and volunteer in civic activities. They will have come through a school system that has served them so that they score above state norms on standardized tests and complete their studies by the time they are 19. Their education will take place in a drug-free, crime-free environment. They will leave feeling that the educational system readied them for life and work and will have confidence in the schools when their children attend.
>
> The students will show no differences in graduation rates, job placements, employer satisfaction, or dropouts on the basis of color, race, creed, sex, religion, or national origin.

Notice the difference between this and a mega-level vision: There are no indicators of societal survival, self-sufficiency, or quality of life, although these might be added.

Putting the mission to work. From the system's mission flows a tangible and agreed-upon common destination. From it,

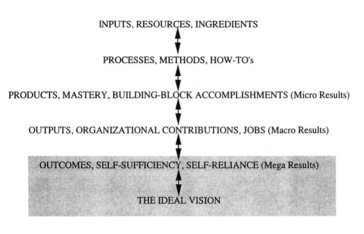

Figure 5.2. The Results (and means) Chain for Macro-Level Planning
NOTE: Mega-level concerns are shown in the shaded area.

we set en route strategic objectives that will move us from current results ever closer to it (and, we hope, toward the ideal vision of mega-level thinking, as shown in Figure 2.3). We construct a results ladder that will link our levels of results, as shown in Figure 5.2.

The achievements of the stepping-stone results may proceed in sequential (and often slow) steps: Micro results might begin to appear this year, and the defined macro results may surface within the next two to three years. For example, if part of the preferred future for our system includes everyone being able to get a job, our schools might achieve that by the year 1997, and graduates and completers will have the requisite skills, knowledge, attitudes, and abilities by 1996, and the component competencies will start to be demonstrated by learners next year. Recall from Chapter 4 that this might have been derived from an ideal vision, such as this one: "Every graduate or completer from the Greater Grise Township schools will be self-sufficient and self-reliant and not under the care, custody, or control of another person, agency, or substance."

Remember, the macro mission should incorporate criteria that allow subsequent objectives and actions to be tangible. The criteria can be used for selecting methods and means to get from our current results to desired ones. Measurable criteria also will allow the partners to evaluate how the system is progressing toward the ideal vision and its system mission.

B. *Relate / Align Beliefs and Values*

Beliefs and values are the perceptual "realities" of the planning partners. Often called by various labels, including "my educational philosophy" or "how I feel about education," beliefs and values usually focus on means, resources, "how-to's." Major assumptions are invariably embedded in these perceptions. The partner's beliefs and values might not be supported by research, but they are frequently treated by each as being close to holy writ. Calling for them to be expressed publicly—Table 4.4 provides a format for identifying beliefs and values—frequently results in emotional responses. Remember that dealing with macro-level objectives is in a not altogether comfortable zone. But encourage people to surface their beliefs and values and allow open and free discussion.

Ask the partners to use the educational system mission (or ideal vision) when stating their beliefs and values. By doing so, self-examination and critical thinking often emerge and allow shifts, modifications, and change. An open and objective discussion concerning beliefs and values is useful. With each person hearing the positions of the others, common directions can be formed.

In guiding the mutual exploration of beliefs and values, an ends/means analysis may be helpful:

1. Collect individual statements of beliefs and values.
2. Extract common and unique beliefs and values.
3. Present the common and unique beliefs and values to the group and ask them to sort each into ends and means.
4. Ask the group to identify those that will contribute to the ideal vision and those that will not.
5. Construct a list of agreed-upon beliefs and values.

C. *Identify Current Mission(s) and Translate Into Mission Objectives*

Most schools and districts have a mission statement. Unfortunately, (a) most people who helped develop it are heavily invested in it; (b) the mission statements are missing measurable criteria for results; (c) the mission statements usually target means and not ends; and therefore (d) they are mission statements and not mission objectives.

Transform the existing mission statement into a mission objective by adding measurable (interval and/or ratio scale) criteria. Recall Critical Success Factor 5: Prepare objectives—including mission objectives—that include measures of how you will know when you have arrived.

At the macro level, the mission objective will include measurable criteria that focus on items of successful learner completion, certification, and exiting to community and society. The relationship between mission statements and mission objectives is in the addition of measurable performance criteria:

mission statement + measurable criteria = mission objective

Table 5.3 provides a format and procedure for translating mission statements into mission objectives at the mega level and for assuring that these relate to the macro and micro levels of results included. Fill out that table (but omit the columns for the mega level, as was required in Table 4.3).

It is essential (in keeping with Critical Success Factors 2 and 3) that objectives deal with ends and that micro- and macro-level objectives be linked.

D. *Identify Needs*

Needs, at least for the purpose of being strategic, are gaps in results, and problems are needs selected for resolution. Needs at the macro level identify gaps in results between current system contributions and required ones. Table 5.4 provides the basic macro-level needs assessment questions.

Figure 4.5 showed the relationship between an ideal vision and current conditions/results, which forms the basis both for the

TABLE 5.3 A Format and Procedure for Assuring That Your Mission Is Useful, Deals with Ends and Not Means, and Has Macro-Level Expectations

| Mission Elements: | Target | | Ends Level | | |
	Means	Ends	Micro	Macro	Mega
a)					
b)					
c)					
etc...					

NOTE: Mega-level considerations are shown in shaded areas. Step 1: List each element of the mission. Step 2: For each, determine whether it relates to a means or an end. Step 3: If an element relates to an end, determine whether it is focused at the micro, macro, or mega level. Step 4: If an element relates to a means, ask "What result would I get if I got or accomplished this?" Keep asking the same question until an end is identified.

identification of mega-level needs and for further planning and accomplishment. Macro-level needs and resulting objectives are those that are shown as closer in than the ideal vision objectives (such as those for the years 2000, 1995, and so on).

After the gaps in results are identified, a needs assessment summary may be constructed. A format for summarizing the needs assessment is provided in Table 3.4 in Chapter 3. Notice again that the first column lists current results, the second lists possible methods and means for closing the gaps, and the third identifies required results. Not ignoring the inevitable methods means (computer-aided instruction, higher teacher salaries, open enrollment) but placing them on the form to wait until each can be linked to a need will dignify the contributions of planning partners. At the same time, it reminds everyone that solutions should only be selected after the needs have been identified and prioritized and the problems selected.

A needs assessment checklist is provided in Table 4.5. After doing a needs assessment, or while work is being done, check off

TABLE 5.4 The Questions That Are the Main Concern of Macro-Level Thinking and Planning

TYPE OF NEEDS ASSESSMENT AND QUASI NEEDS ASSESSMENT FOCUS		QUESTIONS TO BE ASKED AND ANSWERED
NEEDS: Mega/Outcome	#1	Do you care about the success of learners after they leave your educational system and are citizens?
Macro/Output	#2	Do you care about the quality --competence-- of the completers and leavers when they leave your educational system?
Micro/Product	#3	Do you care about the specific skills, knowledges, attitudes, and abilities of the learners as they move from course to course, and level to level?
QUASI NEEDS: Process	#4	Do you care about the efficiency of your educational programs, activities, and methods?
Input	#5	Do you care about the quality and availability of your educational resources, including human, capital, financial, and learning?

NOTE: Note that the mega-level question (shaded area) is assumed or has already been done.

the items. At the macro level, you may omit the column for mega-level needs. A NOM (needs, opportunities, maintenance) assessment (the format was provided in Table 3.5) also may be done at this juncture. For each "what is" and "what should be," identify those needs that should be closed, those critical areas for which there are no gaps *and* there shouldn't be, and areas where there will be gaps in the future if you don't attend to them soon. Also, based upon the system's (macro) mission, identify those areas for which new objectives should be considered.

E. *Identify Matches and Mismatches, Agreements and Disagreements*

There are now hard data (from the needs assessment) and soft data (from the ideal vision). The next vital task is to compare these and identify where the hard data and the soft data agree and disagree (see Figure 4.6).

It is important that different sources of data agree so that the partners will judge the needs assessment data base as useful and will accept the results. Where there isn't accord, initiate further fact finding or reexamine the needs assessment data until you reach agreement.

F. *Obtain Agreement, Reconcile Differences*

Before moving forward, the partners must agree on the needs and assure that the objectives (based on the hard and soft data) agree, are coherent, and will contribute to the achievement of the macro mission. When there are disagreements, help the partners agree. Tools of getting agreement are (a) technical and (b) group process oriented and may be reviewed in Chapter 4.

When disagreement persists, try discussing, listing, and reviewing the historical context and futures data to provide a context for "what was," "what is," "what will be," and "what could be" and finally selecting "what should be." Again, disagreements frequently come from (a) confusing ends and means, (b) insisting on a favored means and not being open to defining gaps in results (needs) first before finding an appropriate means or solution, (c) some people being out of their comfort zone and lashing outward instead of reviewing inward, and/or (d) people playing power games.

Bring these possibilities up with the planning partners and list the existing "needs." Make up a basic chart with the "needs" in a first column and the two other columns marked "ends" and "means." Have the group fill out the chart; they will usually notice that some premature "means" have slipped in and will eliminate them.

G. *Select Long- and Short-Term Missions*

With the attributes of measurable objectives in mind, identify the missions for the future and closer in. Each of these mission objectives should be based upon the shared macro mission, needs, and existing (and now measurable) mission.

Because measurable criteria are used, progress toward each of the near and distant missions—formative evaluation—may be charted and reported. Appropriate responses, resources, and en route changes may be related to the progress. When developing mission objectives, check to assure that each one will make a contribution to the macro mission.

H. *Derive the Macro-Level Mission Objective*

When preparing a system's mission objective, be sure that it has all of the elements of any objective: what is to be accomplished; who or what will demonstrate the accomplishment; under what conditions the accomplishment will be observed; what criteria (ideally interval or ratio scale) will be used.

The macro-level mission objective states where the system is headed and how we will know when it arrives. It is the specification of what the educational system (and its schools, curriculum, and programs) delivers. Evaluation determines the extent to which the results are accomplished based on the mission objective and its detailed criteria.

A hypothetical macro-level mission objective follows:

By the year 2000, at least 95% of all learners entering the Larson School District will graduate and those who want to will get jobs in their first or second occupational choice within six months. Every graduate desiring further higher education will be accepted in a regionally accredited school.

There will be no statistically significant differences among learners in the rates at which they get jobs, score on graduation requirements assessments, graduate, or continue further education because of color, race, creed, sex, religion, or national origin.

There will be a reduction in

- drug-related incidents of at least 96%;

- violence against students and staff of at least 99%;

- dropouts of at least 90%;

- graffiti of 100%;

- learners scoring below the state average on standardized tests for the 11th, 8th, and 6th grades by at least 85%.

The accomplishment of these objectives, and yearly progress toward them, will be certified by the superintendent of schools and approved as correct by the school board.

5.3 Planning

A. *Identify Strengths, Weaknesses, Opportunities, and Threats*

Every educational agency has both strengths and weaknesses, and the agencies don't operate in isolation from the rest of their communities (Kaufman & Herman, 1991a, 1991b). Based on where your educational system is going and the prioritized needs, next objectively identify the system's strengths, weaknesses, opportunities, and threats (SWOTs).

Strengths might include a local research facility for an international computer software company that is willing to provide talent and resources. A weakness might be a political group that opposes sex education. Opportunities could include a new university regional campus moving into the district. And threats might include a new set of federal regulations that threaten vocational programs.

The SWOTs will provide guidance for your decisions as you move from current results toward your mission and macro mission and for building year by year toward achieving each of the close-in and distant mission objectives.

B. *Derive Decision Rules (Results-Referenced Policies)*

Develop results-referenced policies so that everyone within the organization may make decisions that will move toward the missions and the macro mission. Policies should target the achievement of shared results, not compliance. When policies relate to ends, not means, decisions will be made at all levels— from school facilities to board expenditures.

Policies should be public, be stated in simple, clear terms, and avoid legalese. Be ready to modify them when they are no longer useful.

C. *Develop Strategic Action Plans*

This is the heart and soul of being strategic. Based upon the system/macro mission, the priority needs, the close-in and distant mission objectives, the SWOTs, and the policies, the action plan is developed. The plan should include

(a) the macro/system mission;
(b) the mission objectives (including precise performance indicators);
(c) the needs to be addressed each year between now and the most distant mission objective;
(d) the performances that are to be maintained and the opportunities that will be pursued;
(e) the possible methods and means ("how-to's") available to meet each need, as well as those for the selected maintenance requirements and opportunities, and the listing of those methods and means that have been selected;

(f)   the scheduling of human, capital, and physical resources, including required development;

(g)   the budget for each need (or cluster of needs) and the acquisition schedule for each; and

(h)   the evaluation criteria for each need (or cluster of needs).

The macro-level strategic plan should be short and basic. Ten to twenty pages is usually sufficient. A good strategic plan is one that is pulled out and used when decisions are made. Another test of usefulness is whether changes are made to the plan when external reality shifts. If the strategic action plan is thoughtfully developed, and each of the appropriate Critical Success Factors are employed, it will be useful and usable.

After the partners have selected the problems to be resolved and have obtained the budget—but before work proceeds—make certain the partners agree with the anticipated final results. If they do, fine. If they don't, have them recommend modifications and justify revisions.

5.4 Implementation and Evaluation

A. *Put the Strategic Plan to Work*

The strategic plan is useless if not used. So put it to work. Everyone should have a copy of the strategic plan or easy access to one. Each person should know and accept his or her unique role and contributions and know exactly how and when he or she will interact with others to move continuously toward the mission and vision. This cooperation should become a part of the organizational culture. Everyone doesn't have to agree and participate, but those who do not should not be allowed to thwart progress.

B. *Conduct Formative Evaluation*

Evaluation is for correcting, not condemning. We should learn from our experiences and accomplishments, and formative and summative evaluation provide the opportunities for continuous improvement.

Progress toward the missions (and hopefully the ideal vision) should be continuously tracked. When things are developing properly, stay on the track. When there are undesirable deviations, revise as required.

c. *Conduct Summative Evaluation*

The mission objectives (including their performance indicators) furnish the criteria for determining major accomplishments and payoffs. Regular (such as yearly) comparisons should be made on the basis of what was accomplished, and what wasn't. Report what has worked as well as what has not worked. Make recommendations for what to fix, what to keep, and what to terminate.

d. *Revise as Required, and Continue What's Working*

Based upon comparing the results with the objectives, decisions are made on what to continue, what to adjust, and what to stop. Not all methods and means will be successful; even popular ones might be disappointing. Change, add, and drop what isn't contributing to the mission.

Notes

1. Citizenship is usually considered at the macro level but only in terms of providing (giving) the skills and values to be "good" members of society. One useful dimension of citizenship objectives for education is that people, both as learners and community members, will act upon the reciprocal relationship between rights and responsibilities in a democracy. When citizenship is defined in terms of making the world a better place for tomorrow's children, and when curriculum is actually developed and delivered toward that end, then this is a mega-level concern. This equivocal placement of citizenship at one or another level points out that there often is "boundary blur," which makes sharp distinctions between mega-, macro-, and micro-level planning and accomplishment a bit hazy. The functions, however, are more important than the convenient labels.

2. Throughout this chapter, the following terms will be used interchangeably: *macro-level mission, educational system mission,* and *system mission.*

6

Micro-Level Planning: People, Programs, Courses

6.1 When the Primary Beneficiary Is an Educational Organization's Internal Client

Micro-level planning applies to most of what education typically designs, develops, and delivers. Here the primary client and beneficiary are individuals and small groups: an English course, a ninth-grade competency test, physical education teachers, third-grade learners, a special project to improve literacy. Micro-level results are used by internal clients: The teachers of the first grade receive the "products" of kindergarten; the middle school products are "used" by high school teachers.

One does micro-level planning when (a) one has completed mega- and macro-level planning or (b) one is willing to assume that changes and accomplishments at this level will be useful and productive and will roll up from micro-level results to actually contribute to higher-order payoffs.

Much popular interest in schools is focused at the micro level. Parents and citizens ask about standardized test scores, national comparisons on grades and science awards, promotions to next grades. If citizens are interested in micro results, then educators and board members are too. Parents expect their children to take courses, get grades, pass tests, and move through the grades on schedule: a micro focus. We give remarkable attention to grades and test results but rarely place them in a context of how well learners identify and resolve problems, cope and transact with others, or in terms of their success rates as they progress through life.

A. *Micro-Level Planning and Doing: Absolutely Essential*

On the other hand, micro-level accomplishments are unconditionally essential. They are the mortar and brick of education. Regardless of the directions we set at the mega level and the missions established at the macro level, we have to get useful things designed and delivered to learners: This imperative activity occurs at the micro level. Each teacher (or internal client) depends upon the successes of the teachers who worked with the learners before him or her. A weak set of skills acquired in lower grades must be remediated at a later stage or performance will continue to deteriorate.

A primary cause for micro-level actions and consequences being ineffective is when we base them on the wrong objectives. By linking

$$micro \leftrightarrow macro \leftrightarrow mega$$

we can assure what we work so hard at producing will have usefulness both within our schools as well as in life. But nothing gets done in education without action at the micro level.

B. *The Primary Questions to Be Asked and Answered at the Micro Level*

Table 6.1 indicates the micro-level questions. Working at this level either assumes that mega- and macro-level results will surely follow or that work at this level actually builds on mega- and macro-level data.

A micro-level agreement table, similar to the ones provided for the other levels of being strategic, is shown in Table 6.2. Each stakeholder should know what is involved in working at the micro level and should note either agreement or disagreement. Agreement must be obtained to avoid later confusion or arguments.

C. *Relating Strategic and Tactical Planning*

Strategic thinking and planning deal with "what" while tactical planning deals with "how." Because action at this level builds upon actual or implied measurable objectives, and because the primary methods will be applied in school (although it might not be the most cost-effective vehicle), planning at the micro level is more accurately termed *tactical planning*. At the micro level, we are usually identifying instructional objectives, and selecting the most effective ways and means of delivering instruction, rather than being concerned with the overall goals. Usually, changes coming from plans at this level are in the how-to's—tactics—not the whats and whys.

D. *Improving the Products of the System*

It is the intention of micro-level activity to improve the building-block results and contributions of education. Without these results, there will be no systematic or systemic contributions made by educators to learners in our schools and systems.

Much of the literature and work on instructional systems[1] are directed toward improving education (and training) at the micro/product level. Seminars, workshops, and books all give advice on how to improve instructional results. Not only are there useful approaches for performance improvement, but there is addi-

TABLE 6.1 Asking the Right Questions: Seven Basic Questions All Educators Should Ask (and answer)

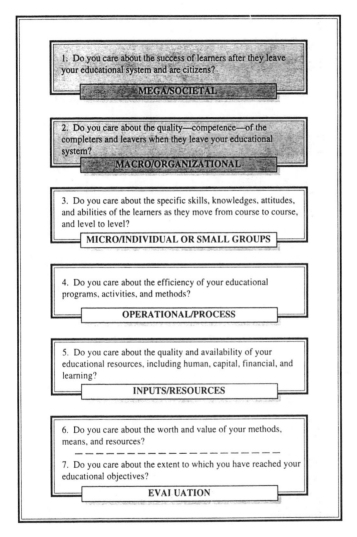

1. Do you care about the success of learners after they leave your educational system and are citizens?

MEGA/SOCIETAL

2. Do you care about the quality—competence—of the completers and leavers when they leave your educational system?

MACRO/ORGANIZATIONAL

3. Do you care about the specific skills, knowledges, attitudes, and abilities of the learners as they move from course to course, and level to level?

MICRO/INDIVIDUAL OR SMALL GROUPS

4. Do you care about the efficiency of your educational programs, activities, and methods?

OPERATIONAL/PROCESS

5. Do you care about the quality and availability of your educational resources, including human, capital, financial, and learning?

INPUTS/RESOURCES

6. Do you care about the worth and value of your methods, means, and resources?

— — — — — — — — — — — — — — — — —

7. Do you care about the extent to which you have reached your educational objectives?

EVALUATION

NOTE: For the micro level, the questions are restricted to 3 through 7.

tional advice for assuring that proper motivational characteristics are included (e.g., Keller, 1983) and that appropriate methods and media are used and linked to learning objectives (e.g., Reiser & Gagne, 1983).

TABLE 6.2 Micro-Level Agreement Table

	Response			
	Stake-holders		Planners	
	Y	N	Y	N
1. All teachers, learners, staff, and parents will contribute to individual learner performance in each of their courses, on special projects and extracurricular activities, and on their individual and national tests.				
2. All courses, programs, and special projects will have measurable objectives that will contribute to 1.				
3. Each course, activity, and its program elements will contribute to 1 and 2.				
4. A needs assessment will identify and document gaps between current results and required results at the performance levels for 1, 2, and 3.				
5. Learning requirements and methods and means for instruction will be generated from the needs identified in 1, 2, and 3 based on the results of 4.				
6. The results of 4 may recommend activities that are not instructional.				
7. All activities, materials, methods, and instructional delivery will contribute to 1 and 2.				
8. Evaluation will use data from comparing results with objectives for 1, 2, 3, and 4, and will identify what is successful and what is to be changed or eliminated.				

We know how to improve individual learner performance measurably. Entire professional societies (e.g., the National Society for Performance & Instruction, AERA, AECT) and journals (e.g., *Educational Technology, Training & Development, Performance & Instruction Journal,* and *Educational Researcher*) are committed to the topic. If we only applied what we knew, we could get measurably improved performance. These improvements and techniques are micro level and are the building blocks of successful education.

The design and development of a successful system have similar features and methods. Strategic planning at the micro level has much in common with instructional systems principles. The phases and steps of strategic planning (Figure 2.1) are the same regardless of the scope selected. Following are the steps of being strategic (or tactical) when the micro level has been selected.

6.2 Scoping

At the micro level, the primary client and beneficiary of what gets planned and delivered is individuals and small groups, such as students taking French courses or special education students. This is the standard choice of teachers, subject matter experts, and evaluators (and will be the most successful when built upon mega-and macro-level plans and data).

All the partners should agree on the micro level of planning and what it will (and will not) deliver. This chapter assumes that the mega and macro levels have been rejected, perhaps only for the moment, or that the higher levels of planning have been done. In case the planning partners are open to reconsidering a premature jump to micro planning, review with them the advantages of mega planning, which were presented in Chapter 4.

To assure that everyone understands that the system intends to work at the micro level, employing an agreement table such as that shown in Table 6.1 may be helpful. Ask each partner formally to accept or reject each proposition. If a planning partner or stakeholder rejects any proposition, he or she assumes responsible for its nonachievement.

A. *Derive the Micro Mission*

After selecting the micro level, derive a mission for the courses and activities within the schools: Define the learning/mastery accomplishments you wish to deliver and what kind of students and performance they will provide.

A micro mission identifies a clear set of results and expectations for what is delivered to internal clients—the learners themselves—as well as how the clients will progress through the system. It defines an intent that enables all partners to become contributing members to the journey. It is written as is any other objective—with the same elements as the ABCD model (Table 3.1). It is crucial that the mission is without any statement of means, resources, and how-to's (e.g., using accelerated learning techniques, equal resources, higher budgets; using teacher aids; following the principles of adult learning theory; using computers). Not that these methods and means might not be selected later, but we should refrain from their selection until we have chosen our destinations and developed measurable criteria for telling us when we have arrived.

The micro mission should not be competitive with another school, set of learners, country, or entity (such as "better test results than Spence School," "more commissioner's scholarships than D'Hemberte Township schools," or "win the brain brawl in the city"). Any mission, including a micro one, should identify a set of precise, measurable, and rigorously defined results. It should project useful results for their own sake, not to keep up with or beat any competition.

An example of a micro mission. A hypothetical micro mission follows:

By the year 2000, all of students in the W & E Swart School will meet 100% of the National Mathematics Teacher's Association standards for math at each and every grade level. In addition, every learner will score at grade level or above on the Rogers Criterion-Referenced Test of Learner Achievement on each subject taught in his or her school, including but not limited to English, Spanish, math, physics, biology, chemistry, art, music, drama, intercultural literature and thought, U.S. history, world history, environment, political systems, problem solving, integrative thinking, and career opportunities. There will be no differences in performance based upon color, race, creed, gender, or national origin. The results will be certified by the superintendent and adopted by the board.

No learner will be convicted of any crime while in the schools, and there will be no graffiti or destruction of school property.

Putting the mission to work. From this mission flows an agreed-upon common and clearly stated destination. From it, we set stepping-stone tactical objectives that will get us from our current results ever closer to future missions (and, if included, toward the ideal vision of mega-level thinking and the missions stated in macro-level planning, as shown in Figure 2.3). We construct a results ladder that will link our levels of results, such as that shown in Figure 6.1.

Continuous improvement as we move toward the micro mission. The achievement of the stepping-stone results may proceed in sequential (and often slow) steps: Component micro results might appear next year, and the component competencies will start to be demonstrated by learners later this year. Each learner and educator in the school and each stakeholder will know where the efforts are heading, agree to the destination, and constantly work, applying their own unique abilities, to get there.

Assure the mission includes measurable criteria. The micro mission must include criteria that allow related objectives and actions to be tangible and provide bench marks for progress. The criteria are used for selecting methods and means to get from the current results to desired ones. Measurable criteria will allow the learners, teachers, and other partners to evaluate how well the system is progressing toward the mission.

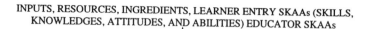

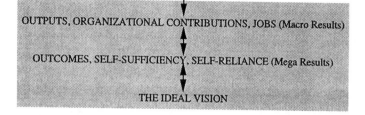

INPUTS, RESOURCES, INGREDIENTS, LEARNER ENTRY SKAAs (SKILLS, KNOWLEDGES, ATTITUDES, AND ABILITIES) EDUCATOR SKAAs

PROCESSES, METHODS, HOW-TO's

PRODUCTS, MASTERY, BUILDING-BLOCK ACCOMPLISHMENTS (Micro Results)

OUTPUTS, ORGANIZATIONAL CONTRIBUTIONS, JOBS (Macro Results)

OUTCOMES, SELF-SUFFICIENCY, SELF-RELIANCE (Mega Results)

THE IDEAL VISION

Figure 6.1. The Results (and means) Chain for Micro-Level Planning
NOTE: Mega- and macro-level concerns are shown in the shaded area.

B. *Relate / Align Beliefs and Values*

Beliefs and values are the planning partner's privately held (perceived) "truths." Often called "my educational philosophy" or "what I know," beliefs and values usually focus on means, resources, and how-to's.

The partner's beliefs and values might not be supported by research or practice, but they are treated as though handed down from on high on marble tablets. Calling for them to be expressed publicly (Table 4.4 provides a format for identifying beliefs and values) can (and frequently does) result in emotional responses and sometimes very emotionally charged arguments.

Recall that dealing with micro-level objectives is in a comfortable zone, but the questioning of beliefs and values might shift this part of the drama to outside the comfort zone of unquestioned paradigms. Agreement and common understandings may be essential, so allow people to surface their beliefs and values and provide for open and objective discussion.

In guiding the mutual exploration of beliefs and values, an ends/means analysis may be helpful:

1. Collect individual statements of beliefs and values.
2. Extract common and unique beliefs and values.
3. Present the common and unique beliefs and values to the group and ask them to sort each into ends and means.
4. Ask the group to identify those that will contribute to their mission (and hopefully to macro and mega results) and those that will not.
5. Construct a list of agreed-upon beliefs and values.

c. Identify Current Mission(s) and Translate Into Mission Objectives

Most schools and districts have a mission statement. Unfortunately, most mission statements (a) have people who are heavily invested and committed to them; (b) are missing measurable criteria, especially in terms of interval or ratio scales, for results; (c) frequently target means and not ends; and (d) are mission statements and not mission objectives.

Translate the existing mission statement into a mission objective by adding measurable (interval and/or ratio scale) criteria. Recall Critical Success Factor 5: Prepare objectives—including mission objectives—that include measures of how you will know when you have arrived. At the micro level, the mission objective will include measurables that deal directly with successful learner completion in school. As at any planning level, a mission objective is made up of a mission statement plus measurable criteria:

mission statement + measurable criteria = mission objective

Table 4.3 provides guidance for translating mission statements into mission objectives at the mega level and for assuring that these relate to the macro and micro levels of results included. If you have completed planning at the mega and macro levels, then continue the analysis. If you have confined your interest to the micro level, fill out that table but omit the columns for the mega and micro levels, as shown in Table 6.3.

Recall that it is essential (in keeping with Critical Success Factors 2 and 3) to assure that objectives deal with ends and

TABLE 6.3 A Format and Procedure for Assuring That Your Mission Is Useful, Deals With Ends and Not Means, and Has Micro-Level Expectations

| Mission Elements: | Target | | Ends Level | | |
	Means	Ends	Micro	Macro	Mega
a)					
b)					
c)					
etc...					

NOTE: Mega- and macro-level considerations are shown in shaded areas. Step 1: List each element of the mission. Step 2: For each, determine whether it relates to a means or an end. Step 3: If an element relates to an end, determine whether it is focused at the micro, macro, or mega level. Step 4: If an element relates to a means, ask: "What result would I get if I got or accomplished this?" Keep asking the same question until an end is identified.

that micro-level objectives will be linked upward to, at least, the macro-level expectations.

D. *Identify Needs*

Needs are gaps in results, and problems are needs selected for resolution. At the micro level, the mission is compared with existing conditions/results, and the identified gaps are the needs.

Figure 4.4 shows the relationship between an ideal vision and current conditions/results that form the basis for the identification of mega- and micro-level needs for further planning and accomplishment. Needs at the macro level identify gaps in results between current course- and activity-level contributions and required ones, as shown in Table 6.4.

Micro-level needs and resulting objectives are those that are shown as closer-in-than-the-ideal and furthest-out objectives (such as for the year 1998).

After the gaps in results are identified, a needs assessment summary may be constructed. A format for a needs assessment

TABLE 6.4 The Questions That Are the Main Concern of Micro-Level Thinking and Planning

TYPE OF NEEDS ASSESSMENT AND QUASI NEEDS ASSESSMENT FOCUS		QUESTIONS TO BE ASKED AND ANSWERED
NEEDS: Mega/Outcome	#1	Do you care about the success of learners after they leave your educational system and are citizens?
Macro/Output	#2	Do you care about the quality --competence-- of the completers and leavers when they leave your educational system?
Micro/Product	#3	Do you care about the specific skills, knowledges, attitudes, and abilities of the learners as they move from course to course, and level to level?
QUASI NEEDS: Process	#4	Do you care about the efficiency of your educational programs, activities, and methods?
Input	#5	Do you care about the quality and availability of your educational resources, including human, capital, financial, and learning?

NOTE: Note that the mega- and macro-level questions (shaded area) are assumed or have already been done.

summary is provided in Table 3.4. Notice again that the first column lists current results; the second, possible methods and means for closing the gaps; and the third identifies required results. Not ignoring the inevitable methods and means (computer-aided instruction, higher teacher pay, equal access), but placing them on the form to wait until each can be linked to a need, dignifies the beliefs and contributions of planning partners at the same time as reminding everyone that solutions should only be selected after the needs have been identified and prioritized and the problems selected.

A needs assessment checklist is provided in Table 4.5. After doing a needs assessment, or while work is contemplated and being done, check off the items at the micro level and omit the columns for mega- and macro-level needs. A NOM (needs, opportunities, maintenance) assessment (see Table 3.5 for the format) may also be done at this point. For each "what is" and "what should be," identify those needs that should be closed, those critical areas for which there are no gaps *and* there shouldn't be, and areas where there will be gaps in the future if we don't attend to them soon. Also, based upon the micro mission, identify those areas for which new objectives should be considered.

E. Identify Matches and Mismatches, Agreements and Disagreements

There are now hard data (from the needs assessment) and soft data (from the mission and any beliefs and values). Identify where the hard data and the soft data agree and disagree (see Figure 4.5). It is important that different sources of data agree so that the partners will perceive the needs assessment data base as useful and will accept the results. Where there isn't accord, initiate further fact finding or reexamine the needs assessment data until you reach agreement.

F. Obtain Agreement: Reconcile Differences

Before progressing, the partners must approve the needs and assure that the objectives (based on the hard and soft data) agree, are coherent, and will contribute to the achievement of the micro (and, directly or by assumption, the macro) mission. When there are disagreements, help the partners come to consensus. Tools of getting agreement are (a) technical and (b) group process oriented and may be reviewed in Chapter 4.

When conflicts persist, discuss, review, and list the historical context and futures data to give a context for "what was," "what is," "what will be," and "what could be" and finally for selecting "what should be." Again, discord frequently comes from (a) confusing ends and means; (b) insisting on a favored means, or solution, and not being open first to defining gaps in results (needs) before finding an appropriate means or solution; (c) some people being out of their comfort zone and getting defensive instead of being reflective; and/or (d) people trying to establish or maintain power.

G. *Select Short-Term Missions*

Using the attributes of measurable objectives, identify the missions for the future and closer in. Each of these mission objectives should be based upon the shared micro mission, needs, and existing (and now measurable) mission.

Because measurable criteria are used, progress toward each of the near and distant missions may be tracked. Appropriate responses, resources, and en route changes may be related to the progress. When developing mission objectives, check to assure that each one will make a contribution not only to the micro mission but also to the macro and mega missions as well.

H. *Derive the Micro-Level Mission Objective*

When preparing a mission objective, make sure that it includes all of the elements of any objective: what is to be accomplished, who or what will demonstrate the accomplishment, under what conditions the accomplishment will be observed, and what criteria (ideally, interval or ratio scales) will be used. Evaluation determines the extent to which the results are accomplished based on the mission objective and its detailed criteria.

A hypothetical micro-level mission objective follows:

By the year 1998, at least 95% of all learners entering the
Larson School District will pass their courses, meet all performance specifications, and move toward graduation
and/or completion within the allotted standard progression
time. All students will score at or above grade level on the
validated national tests of learner progress on all scales
and subjects.

There will be no statistically significant differences
among learners in the rates at which they score on tests,
pass courses, and complete activities on the basis of color,
race, creed, gender, religion, or national origin.

There will be a reduction in

- drug-related incidents of at least 90%;
- violence against students and staff of at least 90%;
- dropouts of at least 80%;
- graffiti of at least 92%;
- learners scoring below the state average on standardized tests for the 11th, 8th, and 6th grades by at
  least 88%.

The accomplishment of these objectives, and yearly progress toward all of them, will be certified by the superintendent of schools and approved as correct by the school board.

6.3 Planning

A. *Identify Strengths, Weaknesses, Opportunities,
and Threats*

Every educational agency has both strengths and weaknesses,
and these agencies don't operate in isolation from the rest of
their communities (Kaufman, Herman, & Watters, in press).
Based on where the system is headed, and the prioritized needs,
objectively identify the system's strengths, weaknesses, opportunities, and threats (SWOTs).

Strengths might include a local educational research facility
for the state university that develops validated school course

software and is willing to provide demonstration materials, talent, and resources. A weakness might be a new board member who is opposed to any automation. Opportunities could include a new technical/vocational regional center being established in the district. And threats might include a new funding formula that threatens after-school programs. The SWOTs will provide guidance for the decisions as you move from current results toward the mission and micro mission and build year by year toward achieving each of the close-in and distant mission objectives.

B. *Derive Decision Rules (Policies)*

Develop results-referenced policies so that everyone within the organization may make decisions that move toward the missions and the micro mission. Policies should target the achievement of shared results, not compliance. When policies relate to ends, not means, decisions will be made at all levels, from school facilities to board expenditures.

Policies should be public and be stated in simple, clear terms and avoid technical terms and "educationese." Be ready to modify them when they are no longer useful.

C. *Develop Strategic Action Plans*

This is the tangible payoff for being strategic (or, at the micro level, being tactical). Based upon the micro mission, the priority needs, the mission objectives, the SWOTs, and the policies, the action plan is developed. The plan should include

(a) the micro mission;
(b) the mission objectives (including precise performance indicators);
(c) the needs to be addressed each year between now and the most distant mission objectives;
(d) the performances that are to be maintained and the opportunities that will be pursued;
(e) the possible methods and means (how-to's) available for each need, as well as for the selected maintenance

requirements and opportunities, and the listing of selected methods and means;

(f) the selected methods and means, based upon instructional
systems principles, and cost-results analyses (what does
it cost to meet the objectives versus what will it cost not
to meet them);

(g) the scheduling of human, capital, and physical resources,
including required development;

(h) the budget for each need (or cluster of needs) and the
acquisition schedule for each; and

(i) the evaluation criteria for each need (or cluster of needs).

The micro-level strategic plan should be basic and provide
only that which operational people have to know and do. Because we are dealing with the details of the delivery of learning
opportunities, this will be longer than the mega- or macro-level
plans. Ten to thirty pages will usually suffice.

A useful strategic plan is one that is used when decisions are
made and one that is changed when external reality changes. If
the strategic action plan is thoughtfully developed, and if each
of the appropriate Critical Success Factors is employed, it will
be useful and usable.

After the partners have selected the problems for resolution
and obtained the budget, but before work proceeds, make certain
the partners agree with the anticipated final results. If they do,
fine. If they don't, have them recommend modifications and justify revisions.

6.4 Implementation and Evaluation

A. *Put the Strategic Plan to Work*

The plan is designed to be used. Everyone should have a copy
of the strategic plan or at least a summary and easy access to a
copy. Each person should know and accept his or her unique role
and contributions and know exactly how and when to interact
with others. This cooperation should become a part of the organ-

izational culture. Everyone doesn't have to agree and participate, but those who do not should not be allowed to derail the plan. Group dynamics should handle all but the most devious, and frustrated, people.

The actual design, development, field testing, revision, and implementation of the instructional system (everything that it takes to meet learning objectives) is part of this step. Again, there are many excellent guides and materials available on what and how to accomplish this (see the References).

B. *Conduct Formative Evaluation*

Evaluation data should be used for continuous improvement, not for punishing. We should learn from our experiences and accomplishments. Formative and summative evaluation provide the opportunities.

Progress toward the missions (and the ideal vision) should be continuously tracked. When things are developing properly, keep going. When there are undesirable deviations, revise as required.

C. *Conduct Summative Evaluation*

The mission objectives (including their performance indicators) furnish the criteria for determining accomplishments and payoffs. Regular (such as yearly) comparisons should be made on the basis of what was accomplished, and what wasn't. Report what has worked as well as what has not worked. Recommendations for what to fix, what to keep, and what to discontinue are made.

D. *Revise as Required and Continue What's Working*

Based upon comparing the results with the objectives, decisions are made on what to continue, what to adjust, and what to stop. Not all methods and means will be successful; even popular ones might disappoint. Modify, add, and delete what isn't contributing to the mission and micro-level mission (and best to the ideal vision).

Key Term

❑ *Tactical planning.* The identification and selection of results to be obtained to meet previously specified (or assumed) objectives; tactical planning usually deals with micro-level results and concerns, such as a single course, activity, or group of students or teachers.

Note

1. Those references specific to instructional systems and performance improvement are identified with an asterisk (*) in the References section at the end of this book.

7

Completing the Plan and Putting It to Work

7.1 Development of the Strategic Action Plan

A. *Function Analysis*

Plans must include the functions—building-block results—to get from today's results to those required by the mission objective. Understanding that all activities and results have to contribute to the common ideal vision mission, a system analysis (Kaufman, 1988b, 1992b) will identify the en route results, or individual contributions, required to make the journey successful.

Briefly, system analysis[1] identifies

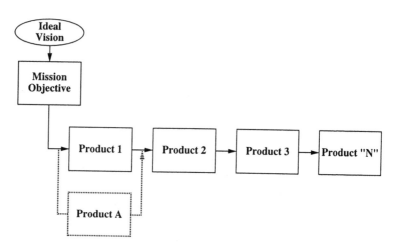

Figure 7.1. A Mission Profile
NOTE: The mission profile (or management plan) identifies the products (or functions) to get from "what is" to the accomplishment of the mission objective. It also shows the order in which they should be completed.

(a) what should be accomplished (the statement of destination is a mission objective, including performance requirements, based upon selected needs);

(b) the building-block "functions" (results, or products) required to get from "what is" to "what should be" (each function has measurable performance requirements); and

(c) the order and relationship among the functions, in a flowchart (also termed a *management plan* or a *mission profile*).

Figure 7.1 identifies, in flowchart (or mission profile) form, the ways in which building-block functions contribute to a mission objective. It also shows, when all of the functions are correctly completed, how they will contribute to the (ideal) vision.

B. *Methods and Means Analysis*

Based upon the derived functions, alternative how-to's are identified so that the most effective and efficient ones may be selected. This identification process is termed *methods-means analysis.* Methods and means are tools, techniques, and/or vehicles for meeting one or a cluster of requirements. A format for methods-means analysis is provided in Table 7.1.

Notice that this format does not select the methods and means, it only identifies them based upon the gaps between current and desired/required results and notes advantages and disadvantages of each.

When identifying possible methods and means, we identify gaps in processes and resources, such as having computers to deliver instruction or the availability of competent troubleshooting instructors. Because we are not dealing with gaps in results, we call these *quasi needs assessments.* (In training and human resource development, this activity is frequently given the deceptive label of *training needs assessment.* It is deceptive because it implies that it is unnecessary to do needs assessments first at the mega, macro, and micro levels to assure the identification and selection of ways and means that are functional, practical, and successful.) Jumping right to a quasi needs assessment violates Critical Success Factor 6.

C. *Methods and Means Selection*

Part of being strategic is selecting the best ways and means to move continuously closer to the ideal vision. A *cost/results analysis* will ask the two simultaneous questions: "What do you give?" and "What do you get?" for each possible how-to (or cluster of methods and means).

Figure 7.2 provides an algorithm for methods and means selection on the basis of a cost/results analysis.

Cost/results analysis techniques—often also called *systems analysis* (*system* analysis deals only with "what"; *systems* analysis deals with "how")—include the following:[2]

- operations research;
- planning, programming, budgeting system (PPBS);
- simulation;
- gaming;

TABLE 7.1 Methods/Means Identification Form

Need Number [a]	Current Performer SKAAs	Required Performer SKAAs	Possible Interventions	Cost/Results Analysis Advantages	Disadvantages

a. Needs may be clustered; several might deal with some common gaps in results.

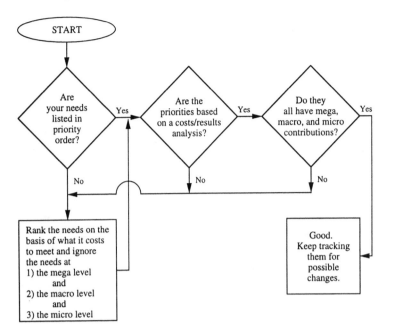

Figure 7.2. Methods and Means Selection Algorithm

- queuing;
- relevance trees;
- Delphi technique;
- nominal group technique;
- polling;
- cross-impact analysis; and
- cycle analysis.

The selected methods and means will identify what programs, projects, activities, classes, courses, and interventions are working; which ones are missing; and which should be dropped. Remember, the identification of functions, possible methods and means, and the selected methods and means are the basis for getting from current results to the accomplishment of the missions.

7.2 Completing the Plan

A. *The Strategic Plan Elements*

It is time to translate the products that the planning partners have worked so hard to create into the actual strategic plan. This is where all the requirements are integrated and put into a single usable document. Following are the suggested sections for this strategic plan report.

Title page. This page should include the specific name of the report, the agency (district, school, agency, consortium), names of the authors, and the date.

Vision. The statement of the ideal vision describes what future the planning partners wish to create. The vision should include indicators of success. (When the vision is relatively short, it can appear on the title page, appropriately boxed.)

Needs. The selected gaps (and anticipated gaps and opportunities) are listed. These provide hard data concerning the realities of current results and desired/required ones. These provide the rationale for the mission objectives.

Educational mission objective(s). This describes the overall agency (school, system, and so on) statement of where it is going and how it will measure when it has arrived. If the mega level has been selected, then the longest-term mission is stated (including all measurable criteria), followed by closer-in missions. Recall Critical Success Factor 4 and make certain that rigorous performance indicators/criteria are included for the mission objective.

Policies. The actual decision criteria that are to be used are listed in this section.

Roles, responsibilities, budgets, and time lines. Individual and group responsibilities for each of the results and missions should be delineated. These are based upon the functions identified during system analysis. This section could include specific programs, projects, and activities.

For each specific function, a measurable objective should be prepared and presented. Time lines for the accomplishment of major functions should also be reported.

Where appropriate, budgets for each mission objective, program, or activity should be reported.

Other elements included here are the management and control elements: How will all of the projects, programs, courses, classes, and support activities be monitored? This management plan may be shown by using organization charts and flow diagrams.

Evaluation plan. This plan describes what will be evaluated and what criteria will be used. An evaluation plan should include both "hard" and "soft" data points and proper assurances that the results and recommendations will be objective.

Appendix. Any required justifications and rationale for the mission objectives and each of the unique interventions, or programs, should be presented here. Especially important will be the presentation of the data-based needs—gaps in results—to show the magnitude of the discrepancies between current status and desired condition. Graphics are very helpful.

B. *If the Plan Is Being Submitted for Approval*

If the plan is being presented for approval, then additional elements should be included:

- the cost to meet each identified need *and* the cost not to meet each need as well as
- alternative costs and benefits for different mission objectives and programs, all related to the ideal vision.

c. *Evaluation / Continuous Improvement*

Evaluation data are used to compare your results with your intentions and decide what to continue, what to modify, and what to discontinue. Evaluation is retrospective, or reactive. It is a vital but after-the-fact determination of successful accomplishment and/or whether or not our methods and resources were appropriate. Unlike strategic planning and its questions (Table 1.2), which are before-the-fact questions, evaluation is only done after interventions have been put into action. Fortunately, evaluation is a lot easier (and rational) when you have been strategic because the evaluation criteria have already been derived as part of planning.

7.3 Management, Leadership, and Operations

Once a plan has been developed and approved, you have to move from concept to application. Managing the educational enterprise is not telling people what to do and then looking over their shoulders to direct them. Management and leadership are getting closer together—moving from supervising to networking, from directing in a hierarchy to finding a common destination and each contributing (Bennis & Nannus, 1985; Drucker, 1973, 1985, 1988; Kanter, 1989; Naisbitt & Aburdene, 1990; Peters, 1987; Roberts, 1987; Senge, 1990; Toffler, 1990; Block, 1993).

The advantage of being strategic is that everyone in the educational system knows

(a) the ideal vision for the society and the system,
(b) the mission objective and all of the performance indicators for telling both direction and destination,
(c) the policies for decisions, and
(d) what each individual and group within the educational system has agreed to contribute.

The elements of leadership and management include commitment to a common destination and to contributing to getting there. Management may now be done by exception: tracking progress toward known objectives, identifying where and when needs (gaps in results) do or might occur, and knowing precisely where to make responsive and responsible changes.

Leaders identify where to go. Managers assure that we get there (Bennis & Nannus, 1985; Drucker, 1973). The new paradigm for education is shared vision, shared mission, and unique contribution—all toward worthy (societal, if the mega level has been selected) ends. *Accountability* now gets redefined as

- agreeing on common destinations and measurable results;
- developing the most effective and efficient ways of getting the required results;
- finding what works, what doesn't, and fixing it—all without blame.

As with all organizations, the success of education depends upon people who work together toward a common end. Adversarial approaches (management versus teachers, teachers versus administrators, parents versus board members) are no-win situations. Power and being dictatorial are *not* the way to get positive results accomplished.

The next section briefly highlights a new (at least for education) approach to leadership and management: *Total Quality Management*. But first, let's put such tools and approaches in context.

7.4 Shifting Our Thinking, Changing Our Organizational Culture

Because some educational agencies might first want to be strategic by applying a Total Quality Management program, this section is presented in stand-alone fashion. Total Quality Management and Total Quality Management Plus (described below) are best used as part of a total strategic approach to education.

A number of management experts argue for the alteration of our thinking and for dramatically changing our organizational cultures (Deal & Kennedy, 1982; Drucker, 1973; Kanter, 1989; Kaufman, 1992b; Peters, 1987; Roberts, 1987; Senge, 1990). The world of education has been plowing along in a rapidly changing world. Not only have the students who come to us changed dramatically, the world in which they live and work is dramatically transforming. Education has to shift its view of its world, clients, environment, and mission as well as how it goes about defining, delivering, and evaluating its services and itself. The education system must rethink how its organizational values and culture must change. There are some frameworks and concepts—first used in the private sector—that can be used.

7.5 Total Quality Management (TQM)

Strategic planning intends to guide us to become more productive in the future. Strategic Planning Plus (SP+) adds the possibility of defining a new future: creating and justifying societally—mega-level—useful objectives that are not being considered. Needs assessments harvest the gaps between current and required results and may be accomplished for the mega, macro, and micro levels of strategic thinking and planning.

Thus there are tools and approaches to improve our future. For a few decades, methods pioneered by Deming and Juran (Galagan, 1991; Kaufman & Zahn, 1993) in the United States and first widely accepted in Japan (because they were outside of the U.S. comfort zone) have shown the way to align people and resources in becoming continuously better—achieving total quality. The process, now being implemented in education, is known by a number of names, the most common being *Total Quality Management* (TQM).

The elements of Total Quality Management. Successes in Japan (which seriously applies TQM), resulting in impressive control of many world markets, have stimulated pleas for education to help make the United States competitive. As businesses are pursuing quality management programs, attention likewise is now turning to the same in education. Both public and private sector organizations are starting TQM initiatives to "do it right the first time—and every time." Not only do organizations realize that they have to define and achieve total quality, there must be continuous improvement in what organizations use, do, produce, and deliver—including educational organizations!

Let's take a brief look at the components of TQM as applied in education, presented in Figure 7.3. Making the resources, methods, products, and deliverables of uniform and consistent high quality—TQM—makes sense. The TQM process is rational, especially if it goes beyond simple "ticket punching" and compliance with arbitrary process-oriented award guidelines. There is growing concern in the private sector that some organizations are missing the point of TQM and are simply jumping hurdles to get an award. How can any organization fail to realize that external clients must be satisfied, which comes from delivering a quality output time after time after time? The issue of taking one's business elsewhere is being seen in the "choice" option, which seems to be a core element of the State and Federal education initiatives. Many nations, including our own, are concerned about the effect of parents sending their children to private schools and about what this does to the effectiveness of the public system given the ethnic/cultural/values mix of those attending the often beleaguered public institutions.

Defining the "Q" in TQM. Output, quality, and customer satisfaction are the vision targets for TQM. Satisfaction comes from everyone in the organization, from sweeper to chief educational officer, working constantly to achieve customer satisfaction. Figure 7.4 shows the elements of the typical TQM process, which rolls up—meshing and integrating—to deliver client satisfaction.

Education can benefit from TQM. We have external clients: the citizens who hire our outputs and pay the taxes. Education has results: products, including learners who complete courses and graduate (or get licenses in a vocational area). In addition, we have processes, those factors of production (we call them "teaching," "learning activities," "curriculum") that deliver results.

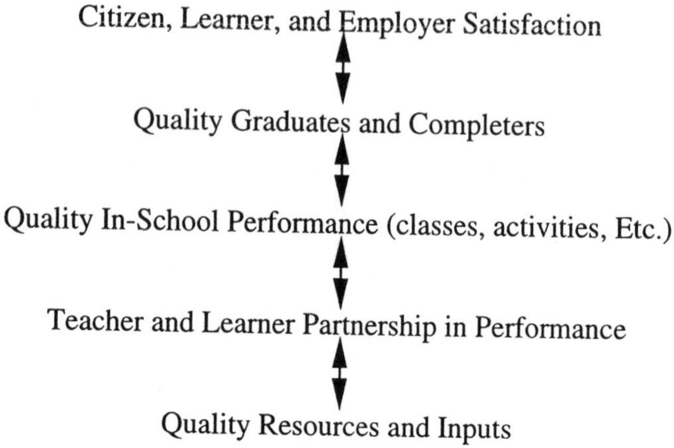

Citizen, Learner, and Employer Satisfaction

↕

Quality Graduates and Completers

↕

Quality In-School Performance (classes, activities, Etc.)

↕

Teacher and Learner Partnership in Performance

↕

Quality Resources and Inputs

Figure 7.3. The Linked Elements in a Conventional Education Total Quality Management Program

And, finally, we have inputs, or ingredients: existing resources, buildings, teachers, and the skills, knowledge, attitudes, and abilities the learners bring to our schools.

Total Quality Management in education links these elements, assuring that they all fit together smoothly and that everyone, including the learners, becomes active and continuous participants in achieving quality. In education, quality consists of the results we deliver: learners who are competent, confident, and can perform on the job. Quality educational outputs (graduates and completers) not only get jobs, but they make a contribution to their organization's clients. In other words, they have the skills, knowledge, attitudes, and abilities to participate in total quality programs where they work.

Do most total quality programs go far enough? All organizations, including educational ones, are means to societal ends, and all have external clients. Education's client list is long and includes almost all communities and members of society.

To keep those external clients satisfied, organizations—including those in education—have to provide value added: a con-

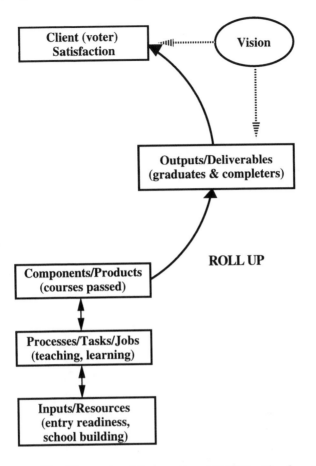

Figure 7.4. The Elements of Conventional TQM (with education-related examples in parentheses)

tinuous positive return on investment. What organizations use, do, develop, and deliver to customers will be evaluated on the basis of *both* customer satisfaction and the usefulness of what is delivered.

Further, then usefulness of outputs is based on the sustained value and worth both to the client and to our shared world. Table 1.2 in Chapter 1 provided the basic questions any organization asks and answers, whether it does so formally or not.

7.6 Quality Management "Plus" (QM+)

A. *Beyond Client Satisfaction*

Peter Drucker reminds us that doing things right is not as important as doing the right things. Total Quality Management, as usually practiced, concentrates on doing things right.

But what about the contributions and usefulness of what satisfies the clients? A few items in the private sector that have resulted in client satisfaction (along with high sales and profits) that turned out to be unacceptable if not downright unhealthy include plastic bags, styrofoam cups/plastic packaging and utensils, chemicals (DDT, Chlordane, some red food dyes), and phosphates in washing detergents.

The missing quality consideration is delivering results that are good for society and that define and create an exemplary world. An ideal vision (see Chapter 3 and 4), in its most functional form, defines a shared vision of not just a successful company, an educational system, and/or a satisfied client. Nor should it be simply a comparative vision intending to compete with another agency or organization; rather, it should identify an ideal—even perfect—condition or world (Senge, 1990).

An "extended" TQM links an ideal vision with conventional TQM—adding the mega level and defining and moving continuously toward the "perfect" world. Figure 7.5 provides a *Quality Management Plus* (QM+) framework. The QM+ process begins outside the organization by identifying what is required for societal usefulness and rolling down to create what should be delivered to the client. It then meets with the roll-up contributions of conventional Total Quality Management. QM+ integrates with and extends conventional TQM.

B. *QM+ in Education: What Can I Do?*

Educators are often the first to realize that something is missing from organizational missions, capabilities, and methods. They see the link between people, productivity, and organizational success but view their posture as reactive and are interested only in their piece of the puzzle (Senge, 1990). When

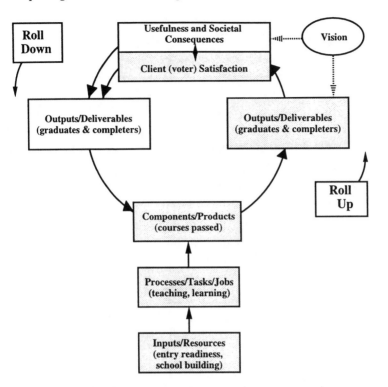

Figure 7.5. The Quality Management Plus (QM+) Cycle
NOTE: Conventional TQM elements are shaded.

developing a TQM program, you might want to open the dialogue with all educational partners about going beyond the conventional framework by adding societal payoffs to client satisfaction. By deriving an ideal vision, and adding that to the standard TQM, your educational system will likely reap a richer harvest. You will be more likely both to deliver total quality and to demonstrate a return on investment in societal terms to learners and taxpayers.

Key Terms

❑ *System analysis.* A rational and systematic process that identifies
   (a) what should be accomplished in terms of a measurable objective (which might be a mission objective) and is based upon selected needs;

    (b)   the building-block "functions" (results or products) required to get from "what is" to "what should be"—each function, because it is results-based, has measurable performance requirements; and

    (c)   the order and relationship among the functions in a flowchart format.

❑ *Systems analysis.* The process for identifying possible ways and means to meet objectives; see *Cost/results analysis.*

❑ *Function analysis.* The identification of the building-block results required to get from current accomplishments to those required by the mission objective: Functions are results—the whats—that, taken together, will deliver a larger result. Function analysis can be in several layers: The sum of each lower level will deliver the higher-level result from which it derives.

❑ *Methods-means analysis.* The process for selecting the best ways and means to get required results; based upon the identified functions, alternative how-to's are identified for later selection.

❑ *Cost/results analysis.* The process for comparing what it costs to deliver a result as compared with the consequences and payoffs of what is delivered. It will ask the two simultaneous questions of "What do you give?" and "What do you get?" for each possible how-to (or cluster of methods and means). Cost/results analysis may be made at each of the three levels of planning: mega/outputs, macro/outputs, and micro/products.

❑ *Total Quality Management (TQM).* One of several labels given to Deming's process for assuring client satisfaction. It is a process, built upon rational data-based decision making, that enrolls everyone in an organization to seek constantly improved quality for what gets delivered.

❑ *Quality Management Plus (QM+).* The extension of TQM to include a focus on the total mega level: current and future societal benefits, not just client satisfaction.

❑ *Evaluation.* The comparison of obtained results and payoffs with intended ones for determining what to keep, what to modify, what to improve and what to discontinue.

Notes

    1. To find out more about the whats and hows of system analysis, please review *Planning Educational Systems* (Kaufman, 1988b) and/or *Strategic Planning Plus* (Kaufman, 1992b). System analysis deals with identifying what should be accomplished and is different than systems analysis, which is concerned with selecting the best "hows."

    2. Those interested in pursuing these techniques are encouraged to consult Kaufman (1988b) and the referenced researchers for each of these tools and approaches.

8

Strategic Thinking in Action

Strategies and tactics can be developed that will measurably improve the world for tomorrow's child. While we are all making the journey together toward the ideal vision, our world will improve.

But there can be obstacles and problems along the way. This chapter addresses what to do when plans appear to be derailed as well as how to keep problems from appearing in the first place. Following are some questions, or issues, that can surface and some advice on how to get things back on track. In addition, references to applicable chapters and useful information are provided.

8.1 Keep Problems From Arising in the First Place

One way to solve problems is to keep them from occurring in the first place. One avenue is to be open to new views and orientations, select the correct destination, and then relate all programs, activities, projects, methods, and resources to that. Another is to define purposes in terms of ends, not means or resources. In addition, defining needs as gaps in results, not as lack of resources or means, also will keep trouble away. Systematic and systemic thinking and planning will provide blueprints for success. (See Chapters 1, 2, 3, and 4.)

Another way to avoid problems is to do what's right—the first time and every time (the basic concept behind Total Quality Management). (See Chapter 7.)

A key tactic for avoiding confrontation, confusion, misunderstanding, and failure is to derive educational activities and resources on the basis of

- an ideal vision;
- agreed-upon beliefs and values (which are compatible with the ideal vision);
- identified needs (not wants);
- mission objectives linking far and near purposes and expectations;
- recognized strengths, weaknesses, opportunities, and threats;
- results-reference policies; and
- strategic action plans that are built upon all of these.

Although there are no guarantees that being strategic will keep all problems away, it will reduce the number that will ambush you. Being strategic includes precision and measurability, the criteria for determining (a) direction and (b) destination. Use this criterion-referenced performance data to revise what should be changed and continue that which is working.

Another advantage to being strategic is the ability to pinpoint problems when they arise. Instead of discovering at the end of a school year or program that something didn't work, formative evaluation indicates what to change before final disaster hits. The measurable criteria from the objectives allow fine-grained analysis of system failure. (See Chapters 3, 4, and 6.)

Important for avoiding problems is building a partnership and building "one team" for defining and achieving educational success. Treat people as partners, not adversaries. There are a number of things you can do to stop people problems before they arrive:

- Be open to others' ideas and concerns. When others know you care about them, they will usually reciprocate. Everyone brings unique experiences, talents, and resources to the planning exercise. Listen and learn along with the group.
- Talk *with* others, not *at* them. Ask for interaction, questions, and ideas.
- Use all six Critical Success Factors (Table 3.7) both for yourself and for the groups with which you work. They define the strategic parameters.
- When convening groups, ask what must be accomplished and avoided.
- Focus on results, not ego.
- Get active participation.

(See Chapters 1 and 2.)

8.2 When Troubles Surface

When problems arise, or when you sense some will, there are some ways to be responsive. The following are some typical situations that may arise and threaten your organizational success and contribution. These issues often interrelate, so don't respond to any one of them in isolation from the others.

(1) "I don't have time for all of this theory! I have kids who are in trouble. I know what they 'need,' and what has to be done. All that's missing are the resources. Why don't we spend the money on kids and not on planning?" The following will help you understand fear: Most people want to do the right thing. There are few really "bad actors" out there. Many who ask this type of question fear the possibility of

- losing control,
- losing face,
- losing territory and/or resources,
- admitting ignorance,
- accountability for something outside of their control, or
- sharing power.

Respect individual comfort zones. By doing so, you are in a position to deal calmly with unstated fears. Listen to people and do the following:

- Allow yourself a different perspective (which may or may not have merit).
- Avoid personal invectives, which are counterproductive. When members feel they are really being heard, they tend to calm down. When not under attack, individuals frequently become more open.

(See Chapters 1, 2, and 4.)

To get to the rationale for being strategic without jumping into quick fixes:

- Use the seven questions (Table 1.2) and ask which ones directly relate to the situation at hand. If this doesn't get people to rethink Questions 1, 2, and 3, refer to Figure 1.3 to help get means and ends practically aligned. Then work through the agreement table (Table 4.1). Share the six Critical Success Factors in Table 3.7.
- Ask the group to list the desired resources and results they will be able to deliver. Go through the results-oriented objectives algorithm (Figure 1.2).
- Ask the group to list the gaps in results that would be reduced or eliminated if (a) their objectives were met and (b) the requested resources were provided. Refer to the needs assessment summary format (Table 3.3).
- Provide them with the needs assessment questions (Table 3.5). Gently keep asking, "If you got the resources and did this: (a) What results would be delivered, (b) What needs would be reduced or eliminated, and (c) What levels—mega, macro, and micro—would be addressed?"
- Remain calm, clear, and open. Don't move faster than their comfort zone shifts (Table 1.5) will allow.

- If only a few of the participants remain intractable, realize you can't "win 'em all." Be patient, and ask them to think about what was just covered as we all keep moving.

(2) "This approach is too cold and impersonal. Not everything can be reduced to measurable results. Let's not forget about people, warmth, caring, and emotion." There is a lot of mythology around nonmeasurability. Refer to Table 3.3 and show how even naming something is measuring. Expand their paradigm concerning evaluation and measurability.

Emphasize that warmth, caring, emotion, and people are important and vital. Point out that these very human and humane considerations are a formal aspect of being strategic and that both "hard" and "soft" data are collected (shown in Figure 4.5 and Table 4.4) and are integrated.

Remind everyone that people are our most important resource, and it is people toward which the entire system is oriented. Go over the importance of Quality Management (Figure 7.3). In addition, success both in school and in life are another added element to caring implementation and management (Figure 7.5).

(3) "This might be OK in the ivory towers, but this isn't the way it works in the real world. Let's get right down to what's really important, and that's courses, learners, content, rigor—and money." This response is also related to problem 1 above. What is more "real world" than preparing learners to improve the world in which they and all others will live. Ask the question, "If you don't derive curriculum, learning, and methods based on what learners have to know and be able to do in today's and tomorrow's world, what do you have in mind?"

- Ask them to identify what level of results and payoffs they do have in mind (Tables 1.2 and 4.1 and Figure 4.1).
- Point out that corporations (worldwide) are increasingly concerned with client satisfaction (Total Quality Management) and even with what is good for both the client and our mutual world (Quality Management Plus).

(See Chapter 7.)

(4) "Those mega-level results and an ideal vision: Education cannot and should not be responsible for all of that! After all, we can only do what we can do; we don't control the learners' world 24 hours a day and shouldn't, even if we could. Shouldn't we just limit ourselves to teaching subjects?" Education is not solely responsible for achieving either the ideal vision or all of the mega-level results. There are other agencies in our world, including the family, health, human services, and labor organizations (to name a few), that can work synergistically with education, as shown in Figure 2.4.

Your educational agency may elect to work with other social and community organizations to contribute, individually and together, to the ideal vision.

Now, about our just teaching courses: Where did we get the objectives for those courses from originally? It is logical to teach learners about subjects that will help them to be successful in school and later life. Figure 1.4 shows how the content of courses can be aligned with current and future realities.

(5) "You can't predict the future, so why pretend? We can teach subjects and courses, and that will really prepare people for the future." Of course, we can't predict the future, but we can help create it. We will all spend the rest of our lives there. If we don't identify the desired future and orient everything we use, do, and deliver to that future, what will happen? If we want a different world, we should define it and attempt to get there. If our preferences change for the kind of world we want for tomorrow's child, we simply change our ideal vision and what we use and do. (Refer to Figure 2.5 and Table 4.1.)

(6) "We've already tried this and it doesn't work." "We already tried management-by-objectives, quality circles, quality management, long-range planning, and even strategic planning. This is going to be just like those—a lot of initial activity, enthusiasm, scurrying around, and then nothing. Why do we have to keep going through these

gimmicks?" We have tried lots of things in the past. All with good intentions. Just look at the extended list of educational reforms that have delivered from slight positive to quite negative results. Understand their frustration and suspicion and acknowledge that there have been many false promises and false starts in the past.

But emphasize this strategic thinking approach is different in key aspects. It is these differences that make it likely to succeed even though others bogged down or faltered. Discuss the six Critical Success Factors (Table 3.7); this isn't "old stale wine in new bottles."

(7) "We've already done needs assessments. Why should we do another one?" Lots of people have done needs assessments, and most of the resulting data are not very useful. Why? They really weren't needs assessments but solutions assessments. Critical Success Factor 6 is often ignored, simply because of the way we commonly use the word *need*. There are a number of different approaches to needs assessment that are being offered and used.

Show them the questions a needs assessment could ask (Table 3.6). Call attention to the needs assessment format (Table 3.4) and write down the "needs" that were uncovered in previous needs assessments. (See Chapter 3.)

Without criticizing previous thinking and efforts, ask the questioner which form of needs assessment he or she feels would be most useful in

(a) identifying useful objectives and achieving the ideal vision;
(b) identifying useful methods and means;
(c) justifying selected resources, methods, and procedures;
(d) justifying what it costs to meet the needs as well as the costs of ignoring them.

If the group is still focused on resources and methods, show how those will be formally considered when doing a methods-means analysis (Table 7.1). (See Chapter 7.)

(8) "We've tried everything. The problems facing education are beyond solution. All we can hope to do is damage control." What a depressing view of our world. Yet there are some who feel that way, that the problems faced are insurmountable, and all we can hope to do is slow down the cancer. It is true, education seems to be resistant to just about every (quick) fix we have tried. And things often do seem to be getting worse. But they really aren't. The past can be only prologue. We can empower ourselves to define and create "what should and will be." Being strategic intends to do just that by asking, answering, and delivering useful results responsive to the strategic questions in Table 1.2.

By asking these questions, committing to answer them, and delivering positive results for tomorrow's child, being strategic can make the difference between a holding action and creating tomorrow.

(9) "How do I prepare a strategic plan?" This entire book is about strategic thinking and planning. When you have to write up a strategic plan, or when you have to let others know what will be in one, review Chapters 3, 4, 5, 6, and 7.

8.3 The Ultimate Education Troubleshooting Tool Kit

The best way to avoid trouble, or to get out of it when you are stuck, is to do the following:

1. Know, use, and apply the six Critical Success Factors (Table 3.7).
2. Know, use, apply, and answer the seven strategic questions (Table 1.2).
3. Be caring, concerned, and rigorous.
4. Be open to change, and correct or stop anything that is not useful.

9

A Hypothetical Case: Strategic Thinking in Sleightown School District

Strategic thinking and planning are practical. They are also very straightforward—once you shift your thinking from "how we always do it around here" to "this is the way we should do it."

To demonstrate how strategic thinking might work in your system, this hypothetical case tracks an application. Sections of the book that relate to specifics in the case are referred to in parentheses.

9.1 The Assignment

This morning. Associate Superintendent *Jane Smythe* came into the office at 7:15 a.m., a bit later than usual. The board meeting the night before was long and contentious. Things haven't been altogether smooth lately. National media coverage has been showing the schools to be crime ridden, slothful, wasteful, and the cause of our lack of international competitiveness.

State funding has been behind inflation for several years, and although there have been outcries for excellence and accountability (again), there are more directives than cash. To cap things off for Sleightown, there was a mugging on the school grounds in one of the better neighborhoods, and two of the board members (also up for reelection) are calling for "blood." Today was to be spent picking through all of the board's instructions and trying to get some education done as well. After all, somebody has to look after the children.

The board and superintendent. The board is made up of basically decent people, but they tend to get involved in one single-issue quick-fix solution at a time. Last year, the emphasis was on reading and literacy; several years before, it was excellence; and this year, it is fiscal responsibility and accountability. Their appointed superintendent, *Dr. Tam Schandley*, is a caring professional educator, a former teacher, principal, and assistant superintendent.

The school system. But things aren't getting better. Good teachers are too often leaving. Test scores (after declining for several years) are now stable, drug use is level, but alcohol consumption is increasing as are vandalism and gambling. There are ethnic problems surfacing, such as some high school students—of different races—demanding segregated proms. Roving gangs often spill into some of the schools.

The conditions in the school are not nearly as serious as most parents believe, but day-to-day publicity of everything that goes wrong doesn't begin to allow people to understand how much right there is with the system. Kids do learn, many go to college, and the curriculum does allow useful and productive citizens to emerge. Most well-to-do parents disbelieve these facts, and a number did send their offspring to private schools. Everyone wants change, but each has his or her own opinion of what the change should be.

Last night, the board, not unmindful of the forthcoming elections, voted to "achieve excellence in our schools and to raise test scores until they were above the state average." They called the initiative "total quality accountability."

A typical school system in a typical community: Everyone knows that education is important, but they differ on how to deliver it, thus causing confusion, conflict, and frustration.

The new assignment. Tam invited Jane into his office and got right down to business. "Jane, we are sitting on a quietly ticking time bomb. We both know that this new board initiative will just have us spinning our wheels, and it only provides ammunition for attack. There's nothing in here for teachers or kids, and this just can't go on year, after year, after year." Jane nodded her head. Tam and she often agreed, although she was the one who always got things done.

"I want you to lead us in strategic planning, or long-range planning, or whatever you call it. I want to have a blueprint for this system that will give us clear and justifiable directions. Our board retreats end up being nothing more than a yearly work plan and budget, and I want a real plan to set our direction for years to come."

Jane already had enough to do, but she immediately realized that the idea she planted two years ago was about to take root. "Right!" Jane returned to her office. Her head raced concerning how she was going to attack the assignment and find a model that suited her district, not her consultants.

9.2 Planning to Plan

Doing her homework. She called the high school principal and the principal at Southside Elementary. She told them what she was up to and asked for their input, cooperation, and counsel. They expressed doubts that this exercise would be different, to which Jane told them, "It will be if we do it right; if we are bold enough to break the mold, and if you will commit to help me make it real and useful." They bought in.

Asking the right questions. Jane sat down and listed what a strategic plan had to accomplish. She thought, "Let me write down the questions we want answers to. If strategic planning is the solution, what are the problems?" If she could pose the right questions, she thought, then she could relate all of the models and approaches to those and find out what would be useful for Sleightown's schools.

She asked herself, "Who really are the clients of what Sleightown schools use, do, and deliver? Students? Teachers? Parents? Employers?" The quick and conventional pick was the learners, but she hesitated. She recalled her time as a teacher and principal and how she always had to relate to the community.

"If Sleightown schools are the solution, what's the problem?" Immediately it became clear: The primary client of the school system was the society and the community, now and in the future. "I bet the reason we have all of the conflict and are getting poorer results is that we have never really identified our goals and objectives on the basis of improving our world, and the world in which our learners will live and contribute! We've been teaching subjects, and not learners!" Jane started writing. The questions (Table 1.2) flowed, and she came up with her questions for strategic thinking (and planning):

1. Do we care about the success of Sleightown learners after they leave our system and become citizens?
2. Do we care about the quality—competence and abilities— of our system's completers and leavers?
3. Do we care about the specific skills, knowledge, attitudes, and abilities of our learners as they move from course to course, and level to level, within the Sleightown system?

4. Do we care about the efficiency of our educational programs, activities, and methods?
5. Do we care about the quality and availability of our resources, including human, financial, and learning capital?

These seemed important, all right. They were what we should
be concerned about *and* commit to. But these were all about
planning. Don't we require some questions about evaluation?

6. Do we care about the worth and value of our methods,
   means, and resources? Do we care about what works, and
   how well?
7. Do we care about the extent to which we have reached our
   objectives?

Jane knew the questions were pretty close to right. And she
knew that they would bother some of her associates, especially
Question 1. These kinds of questions, and this almost larger-
than-life framework, would move many people out of their comfort zones. When people get their paradigms (see Chapter 1 and
Table 1.5) and operating ground rules challenged, they usually
do one of several things: don't let the changes "in," distort them
to fit with the ways in which they feel comfortable working, consider change, or get hostile. To get results, she had to enroll all
of the educational partners.

Jane took Tam off to a quiet conference room and let it all fly.
At first, he was concerned, for he was smart enough to realize
what Jane was proposing and also politic enough to realize that
these questions, especially the first two, were far different than
those that would be comfortable for the board, the media, and
the most of the staff.

"Tam," Jane said, "you know this is right. It might not be comfortable, but it's right." Tam sighed. He knew he was at a choice
point. "Dammit, Jane," blustered Tam, "why do you have to be
right! You make me choose between what's good for kids and
what's comfortable for me. Let's go for it!" Jane knew she was
launched and also realized that the trip into orbit would have
some jostles and bumps.

9.3 Selecting the Strategic Framework

Jane was splitting her energies now between doing her "administrivia" and getting the planning on track. She made a mental note: If we had been acting strategically in the past, we would know exactly how to handle these problems that seem to be constantly washing over us.

She got a book (this one) on strategic planning. The author called the approach "Strategic Planning Plus" and the "plus" was mega planning (Question 1 in Table 1.2), where the primary client and beneficiary of what gets planned and delivered is the society of today and tomorrow. There's a match.

Jane reviewed the three-phase strategic thinking and planning framework—scoping, planning, implementation and evaluation/continuous improvement (see Chapter 2 and Figure 2.2)—and realized that she had her blueprint. It was all so simple, but others would see it as complex at first.

9.4 Strategic Thinking and Planning Begin

Selecting the planning partners. She identified the planning partners (see Chapter 2)—those who would represent the educational stakeholders of learners, teachers, principals, guidance counselors, clerks, maintenance, bus drivers, cooks, parents, and community members—and consulted with her associates, especially the principals, to make sure she had all of the bases covered. The board decided not to have every individual member become a planning partner but elected two of their members. Jane insisted that one principal, one teacher, and two students would be among the planning partners. And no "professional troublemakers," either, were to be planning partners. Jane next obtained the commitment of those who would serve. She told them what was expected and that their contributions would form the plan.

They held their first meeting. Jane discussed the phenomenon of comfort zones and paradigms frankly: Critical Success Factor 1 (Table 3.7). The planning partners were surprised, but open.

***The planning group gets to work and starts thinking
strategically.*** Jane had each of the planning partners introduce him- or herself and identify the one *result* the strategic
plan would have to deliver and the one *result* it must not render.
At each introduction, Jane wrote the musts and must-nots down
and later had the group designate each as a "means" or an "end."
All were surprised at how means oriented they were and thus
provided the opportunity for her to introduce Critical Success
Factor 2 (Table 3.7): Differentiate between ends and means (between what and how).

There was some puzzlement, but soon most people got comfortable with the means/ends distinction. Jane used the opportunity to talk about the three different levels of results and
introduced Critical Success Factor 3 (Table 3.7): Use all three
levels of results (mega, macro, and micro). Together, they sorted
the planning partners' musts and must-nots and found that not
only were there very few results at the mega level, there were
many resources and processes that were confused with ends.

Some confusion reigned, but all still seemed to be open. A couple of people kept insisting that a (favored) means was really an
end. Jane asked them to relate their positions to ends and
means, and although most people realized right away that these
people were hanging on tenaciously to means, the proponents
got a bit abusive and tried to label Jane (behind her back) as
offensive. Jane reviewed the Critical Success Factors (Table 3.7,
especially 1) and decided that the group, with a few exceptions,
would appreciate moving on.

Jane showed the group the seven important "strategic" questions (Table 1.2), and asked, "Which questions can we ignore?
And which ones do we currently only pay lip-service to?" They
took another discussion break, and most people decided that all
of the questions had to take center stage. They also had good
agreement that everyone tended to talk about Question 1 but
really didn't factor it into thinking, planning, and evaluation.

It was time to develop an ideal vision. Jane showed them that
an ideal vision (Chapter 2) concerned the mega level and that
we shouldn't limit ourselves to what we knew we could deliver
but that the task was to describe the kind of world we want for
tomorrow's child.

Two splinter groups lobbied to be "here-and-now" practical. About a quarter of the group (including one teacher and a student) decided that this activity was too, well, "utopian" and impractical, and wanted to get right down to the here and now. One splinter group wanted to start developing a vision for courses, grades, test scores, values, and discipline, and another fragment group wanted to work on graduation and getting jobs.

Yet most—about three quarters—of the planning partners wanted to develop the ideal (mega-level) vision. It was decided that there would be three planning groups for now, one for each of the possible planning scopes: One would work on macro-level missions (Chapter 5: graduation, job placement), another on micro-level interests (Chapter 6: course grades and test results), and the larger group would continue on at the mega level.

The ideal vision developed. An ideal vision (Chapter 4) was next developed by the mega-scope group. They asked for some examples, and Jane also gave them a format to use (Table 4.2):

The world will be at peace, with no murders, rapes, crimes, violence, or substance abuse. Nobody will die from infectious disease, and every child will be a wanted child. Poverty will not exist, and all persons will earn as much as it costs them to live unless they are going to school and moving toward preparing themselves to be self-sufficient and self-reliant. The disadvantaged will be helped to help themselves and become increasingly close to being self-sufficient and self-reliant. People will take charge of their lives and be responsible for what they use, do, and contribute. Loving and caring partnerships will form and sustain themselves. Government's contribution will be assisting people to be happy and self-sustaining, will reinforce independence and mutual contribution, and will be organized and funded to the extent to which it meets its objectives. Business will earn a profit without bringing harm to its clients and our mutual world. No species will go extinct and everyone will have clean air to breathe, water to drink, and food to eat. There will be no discrimination among peoples, and there will be no differences among people on the basis of color, race, creed, gender, age, religion, or national origin.

A few thought this would be a tall order. "Impossible," mumbled a pair. Jane reminded them that this was the ideal for our shared world, and the team would have to define the part of the ideal for which they would become responsible for (Figure 2.4). When they heard this, they were ready to develop the mission objective for the district. Jane told them about Critical Success Factor 4 (Table 3.7): Prepare objectives—including mission objectives—that include measures of how you will know when you have arrived. She also reminded them of the three levels of results and the ends/means distinction: Critical Success Factors 2 and 3 (Table 3.7).

Beliefs and values. "But first," said Jane, "we have to deal with our beliefs and values, to make certain we all understand each other and that we all will commit to moving toward the ideal vision." One partner noted, "We already have been dealing with our beliefs and values, haven't we? I think a lot of the arguments, especially the ones you showed us were means, were really our values showing." She provided them with a format (Table 4.4) and they got right down to work.

They came up with a list, discussed the items, and wrote them out. They used the ends/means comparison again and were quite surprised to find out how many of their items were (a) means or resources oriented and (b) were really not rooted in actual data. It was a revelation to some and a threat to others. Yet, they came up with a list. They broke for the day.

The next day, Jane told them, "We have to identify needs—the gaps between current results and consequences and the ideal vision." She provided them with an algorithm for stating needs and relating them to the three levels of results (Figure 3.1) and a needs assessment summary form (Table 3.4). Many said they realized that, at least for planning, needs are gaps in results, but then they kept saying things like "we 'need' to have more contact hours and time on task," and "we 'need' to hire more teachers." When Jane wrote these statements (actually premature selections of means) on the board and asked everyone to state whether they were means or ends, the realization "hit."

Some started getting restless; a couple of them even got defensive. "Don't dictate to me what I say or do," and "I, and everyone else, knows what I mean when I say 'need'!" "Oops," noted Jane, "we have gotten a bit out of our comfort zone, haven't we?" Some vigorous discussion went on, and Jane walked the partners through the processes using the job aids. They finally understood about the importance of using *need* as a noun—a gap in results, not in processes or resources—and that was a logical extension of Critical Success Factor 2 (Table 3.7).

The partners appointed three people to go to the central office and get the data on the gaps between the ideal vision and current results and payoffs.

Working on the Sleightown Schools mission statement.

In the meantime, the rest of the mega-level group took the current mission of the system and made it measurable. They realized that the board-adopted mission statement was not really very precise or not at all societally focused.

The group decided first whether or not the mission statement dealt with ends or means (Table 4.3) and then what level of results (mega, macro, micro) were targeted. They smiled at each other knowingly; this mission statement, which seemed so comfortable each year the board readopted it, seemed so, well, naive. The group was well into thinking strategically. They broke for lunch, wondering how the needs-data gathering excursion was going.

Reporting on needs.

They were surprised when the needs-data gatherers were back right after lunch with the data. The three noted that, when they asked specific questions (based on the criteria from the ideal vision), so much data were available. They reported their findings, and the gaps in results were plotted on the board in front of the group. Some of the data were surprising, such as the real number of dropouts/push-outs (31%!), births to unmarried and teenage mothers (6% of the female students!), and those going on to higher education who wanted to (63% going versus 88% who wanted to go). Other data were within the ballpark, including the number scoring at or above national averages on tests (63%, with an unhappy 23% below on math and science) and the number who were graduating or receiving vocational-technical certificates (91%).

For each data point (related to the first three strategic questions), the group selected the "what should be." A list of needs were derived, and they aligned with the strategic questions (Tables 1.2 and 3.6). Several planning team members noted that there were not any needs relating to the environment, or mutual world survival and peace, and these were added to the possible "opportunities" (Table 3.5). For several data points, the group decided that, while there were no gaps in results, none should be allowed to develop; this level of performance should be maintained. Everyone in the mega-level group was pleased.

Getting together with the splinter groups. But things were not completely together yet. The two minority-opinion groups had not been yet heard from nor were their inputs resolved and integrated. Silently, most of the mega partners wished they could go ahead without them. But, with Jane's leadership, they realized that strategic thinking was for everyone, not just those who felt comfortable with it.

They (now outsiders) were invited back. They looked like they had gone through a wringer. Each of the two groups reported, and they sadly noted they had not made much progress. The macro-level group agreed that everyone should graduate or complete but had gotten bogged down in how that could be accomplished and exactly what the graduation requirements should include. The micro-level group had agreed on an objective that at least 80% of all learners would get a grade of C or better in 90% of their courses but again disagreed on how to get that done and on exactly what courses should be in the curriculum.

Jane suggested that perhaps they had been exposed to enough strategic thinking that they were uncomfortable with the old ways. "And," she noted, "your differences on what should be accomplished can probably be resolved by the ideal vision being used as a common guiding star—a common destination." The members of the splinter groups looked at each other and then looked back intently at Jane.

Identifying matches and mismatches and reconciling differences. "Let's go over what your other planning partners were doing, and I think you will find out that we have been going down parallel tracks the whole time." Jane had the mega partners present their ideal vision, needs, and measurable indicators (and concerns about) the existing Sleightown District mission. The splinter group members looked relieved and voted to join with the mega partners "just so long as our work isn't overlooked or forgotten." Jane took their written statements and taped them up conspicuously in front.

Jane noted that they all had now gone through the roughest rapids, and the water would be a lot smoother from now on—at least for the planning partners. It was time for another break, this time overnight.

Setting mission objectives, including at the mega level. Now it was time to write a measurable objective to state what the district would deliver to the citizens who paid for education in Sleightown. Jane gave them the elements of a measurable objective (Table 3.1), as well as an algorithm for writing measurable objectives (Figure 4.6), and put the ideal vision up in front of the group. She also displayed the beliefs and values that had been derived and reconciled the day before.

The groups worked hard, and it was especially difficult to keep methods and means (money, teacher credentials, subjects, values education) out of the objectives, but, after several rounds, they had a mega-level mission objective, based on what they agreed the Sleightown schools should contribute to it:

> By the year 2000, our community will have at least a 90% lower rate of (a) teenage and unwed mother births; (b) drug-related crimes on and off school grounds; (c) families living in poverty and/or living in mental institutions; (d) reported AIDS cases and cases of other preventable infectious diseases; and (e) murders, rapes, or crimes of violence.
>
> At least 95% of all learners will graduate or be awarded a competency-based vocational license, and at least 95% of those will get and keep jobs of their first or second occupational choice or attend an accredited institution of higher

education. Of those working, every woman and man will earn as much as it costs them to live. At least 90% of employers of the districts' learners will rate them above average or better on their competency and contribution to the company's objectives and clients. Those not graduating or completing will be helped to help themselves so that they are increasingly close to being self-sufficient and self-reliant (as indicated by an increase in the amount of money their work produces and contributes to their subsistence, and so on). Family partnerships will form and sustain themselves (as indicated by an at least 80% decrease in district citizens' divorce rate, no judgments of physical abuse for persons living together, and so on).

The superintendent will cause to be derived valid and measurable criteria for these intentions, have them validated by an independent expert, and certify the results each year between next January 2 and the year 2000. In addition, at least once yearly, the superintendent will report on, and make recommendations for, objectives that should be added to the mission objective as well as those that should be deleted and/or modified. Finally, the superintendent's report will describe progress toward the ideal vision. The results and recommendations will be accepted as correct by a board vote.

The group invited the superintendent and the board chairwoman to hear their mission. After some requests for clarification (and the board chair challenging why there weren't resources mentioned at all), Tam approved of the mission and the work to this point.

Everyone was tired and wanted to adjourn. Concerned that people might forget some major Critical Success Factors and the growth that had occurred, Jane suggested that some of the group do some "homework" for the next meeting. Five people agreed to take what had been developed and identify Sleightown's SWOTs: strengths, weaknesses, opportunities, and threats (see Chapter 2).

Identifying the strengths, weaknesses, opportunities, and threats (SWOTs). When the entire team got back together

(Jane had met with them in between) in three weeks, they shared their thoughts on what had been developed, and most were pleased with their progress and status. Others wanted more rigor in the performance specifications for the mission objective. Then the SWOT team presented their SWOTs, and most were accepted. The only real argument was whether the national direct-to-district funding of special education and some vocational training was a "threat" or an "opportunity." Jane shared that most threats were really the opening for possible change and thus, with hard and innovative work, could be turned into opportunities.

Deriving decision rules—policies. The next piece of work was to develop results-based policies. Most of the planning partners felt that was the business of the central office and asked them to make them up and report back. Jane, somewhat reluctantly, agreed, and Jane's assistant Phil agreed to take on the task.

Early the next morning, he provided a tentative list of policies and the mission objective elements for each year between then and the year 2000, to which they contributed. Everyone was impressed and, with a few modifications, accepted Phil's work.

Developing the strategic action plan. Now to the "meat" of the entire effort—developing the plan. Jane shared what she thought should be in the plan, including a format (Chapter 7), and they went to work. After several small and large group consultations, the pieces started to emerge.

Title page: "Strategic Plan for the Sleightown Schools. Prepared by the Sleightown Strategic Planning Partnership [complete roster on inside cover]. November."

Vision: They listed the ideal vision they had derived, with indicators of success.

Needs: They listed the selected gaps and anticipated ones. They also identified some possible future opportunities in the areas served by the existing schools. These provided hard data concerning the realities of current results and desired/required ones.

Educational mission objective(s): The overall Sleightown mega-level mission objective for the year 2000, and for each year between then and now, is listed. They also included all measurable criteria for each of the mission objectives.

Appendix: They noted that the rationale for each of the objectives was to be found in an appendix.

Policies: The actual decision criteria to be used were listed.

Now, before going on to the gritty part of the plan, it was time to get together with the professional staff. They scheduled a meeting a week hence, provided the staff with what they had developed, and let them know that the detailed plan would be co-created.

They adjourned for a week while the central office staff pored over the plan, its elements, and what they had to help create. Some were clearly nervous.

Getting staff commitment. Jane scheduled a meeting with the staff and representative teachers and students and walked them through the basics of strategic thinking and planning. They reacted pretty much the same way that the planners did, and Jane handled it the same way; educators are really a microcosm of the larger community. It was fortunate that they had been represented on the planning committee, for, if they had not been, the entire process could have been jeopardized.

Bringing everyone together: One team. A newly constituted team met a week later, this time with educators and learners represented. Jane told the entire group of her error, asked them to approve of the newcomers, and held her breath. They laughed a little, realizing that they too had neglected to recognize the importance of a true partnership, and welcomed all. Jane was relieved. It was time to continue.

Roles, responsibilities, budgets, and time lines. They broke up into groups to do a function analysis for what results (not means or methods) were required to get from where the district was (based upon the needs) to where it should be headed. They did a function analysis (Figure 7.1) and then identified what the alternative ways and means were to get each function accomplished (Chapter 7 and Table 7.1).

Then they did a methods-means selection (Figure 7.2) but felt uncomfortable with it because most of the people involved were not professional educators. They leaned increasingly on the educators who had been added late to the group, but because there was an agreed-on ideal vision and mission objectives, they were comfortable with the plan that was developing.

The group, with the financial officer, developed the budgets and time lines: schedules of functions and results with associated resources that would get from one sequential building-block objective to the next until each mission would be reached. Also derived was a list of human, physical, and capital resources both on hand and required. For each function, the necessary resources were listed along with what was missing and what it would cost to acquire the missing resource.

New programs were identified, primarily by the district's educational specialists. Others programs were to be modified, and still a few were slated to be discontinued.

A management plan was developed, showing how more and more staff would be empowered to make decisions (based upon the results-based policies) and how school-based management could finally be made to work—now that everyone had a common North Star toward which to steer. Of special interest was the organization chart; they had developed a circular one with society in the center, learners in the next ring, and then functions and delivery specialists around that.

Because the plan had to be approved by the board, and because it was sure to get much newspaper scrutiny, additional elements were included:

- Cost to meet each identified need *and* the cost not to meet each need
- Alternative costs and benefits for different mission objectives and programs, all related to the vision

Evaluation plan. The planning partners provided an evaluation plan, including the mission objectives and performance requirements that would be used to provide data on what was working and what was not. They indicated that there was to be both an internal formative (continuous improvement) evaluation and an independent assessment of programs, projects, courses, and accomplishments.

Also included in the evaluation plan was an assessment of what learners, teachers, parents, community members, and employers thought of what Sleightown's schools were delivering and contributing.

9.5 Implementation and Evaluation

The planning group had done its job—and well. They had formed a new future and a new partnership. The new objectives were toward creating a better and better world for tomorrow's child. And everyone knew where the system was headed, knew why, and was committed to continuously improve it.

Appendix. The rationale for the mission objectives and for the different initiatives was provided here. Especially noted were the "hard" data to demonstrate the gaps in results (such as dropout rates compared with objectives) for each mission objective.

9.6 Getting the Plan Accepted and Implemented

The plan was submitted to the board. It was approved on a 5-2 vote. Tam held a meeting with the central office as well as with all school administrators and department heads and agreed on the functions, times, and resources.

Jane is taking a well-deserved week on a beach in Hawaii.

References
and
Related Resources

(Those references with an asterisk [*] are references specific to instructional systems design and development.)

America 2000: An education strategy. (1991, April 18). Washington, DC: US Department of Education Sourcebook.

*Banathy, B. (1987). Instructional systems design. In R. M. Gagne (Ed.), *Instructional technology: Foundations.* Hillsdale, NJ: Lawrence Erlbaum.

Banathy, B. H. (1991). *Systems design of education: A journey to create the future.* Englewood Cliffs, NJ: Educational Technology.

*Banghart, F. W. (1969). *Educational systems analysis.* Toronto, Ontario: Macmillan.

Barker, J. (1989). *The business of paradigms.* [Videotape]. Burnsville, MN: Charthouse.

Barker, J. (1993). *Paradigm pioneers.* [Videotape]. Burnsville, MN: Charthouse.

Bennis, W., & Nannus, B. (1985). *Leaders: The strategies for taking charge.* New York: Harper & Row.

Bertalanffy, L., Von (1968). *General systems theory.* New York: George Braziller.

Bhote, K. R. (1989). The Malcolm Baldridge Quality Award. *National Productivity Review, 8*(4).

Block, P. (1993). *Stewardship.* San Francisco: Berrett-Kochler.

Branson, R. K. (1987). Why schools can't improve: The upper limit hypothesis. *Journal of Instructional Development, 4*(10).

Branson, R. K. (1991, April). *Restructuring public education: Imagining, visioning, or reforming?* Paper presented at the annual meeting of the American Educational Research Association, Chicago.

*Branson, R. K., et al. (1975, August). *Interservice procedures for instructional systems development (Phases I, II, III, IV, V, and Executive Summary)* (U.S. Army Training and Doctrine Command Pamphlet 350). Fort Monroe, VA: U.S. Army.

*Briggs, L. J. (Ed.). (1977). *Instructional design: Principles and applications.* Englewood Cliffs, NJ: Educational Technology.

*Carlson, R. V., & Awkerman, G. (Eds.). (1991). *Educational planning: Concepts, strategies, practices.* New York: Longman.

Carnoy, W., & Levin, H. M. (1976). *The limits of educational reform.* New York: David McKay.

Carter, R. K. (1983). *The accountable agency* (Human Service Guide No. 34). Beverly Hills, CA: Sage.

Churchman, C. W. (1975). *The systems approach* (2nd ed.). New York: Dell. (First edition published 1969)

Cleland, D. I., & King, W. R. (1968). *Systems, organizations, analysis, management: A book of readings.* New York: McGraw-Hill.

Conner, D. R. (1992). *Managing at the speed of change.* New York: Villard.

Cook, W. J., Jr. (1988). [A series of four videotapes in association with *Strategic Planning for America's Schools*]. Arlington, VA: National Academy of School Executives and the American Association of School Administrators.

Cook, W. J., Jr. (1990). *Bill Cook's strategic planning for America's schools* (rev. ed.). Birmingham, AL: Cambridge Management Group, Inc.; Arlington, VA: the American Association of School Administrators.

*Corrigan, R. E., & Corrigan, B. O. (1985). *SAFE: System approach for effectiveness.* Anaheim, CA: R. E. Corrigan Associates.

Corrigan, R. E., & Kaufman, R. (1966). *Why system engineering?* Palo Alto, CA: Fearon.

Cuban, L. (1990, January). Reforming again, again, and again. *Educational Researcher,* pp. 3-13.

Deal, T., & Kennedy, A. (1982). *Corporate cultures: The rites and rituals of corporate life.* Reading, MA: Addison-Wesley.

*Dick, W., & Carey, L. (1989). *The systematic design of instruction* (3rd ed.). Glenview, IL: Scott, Foresman.

Drucker, P. F. (1973). *Management: Tasks, responsibilities, practices.* New York: Harper & Row.

Drucker, P. F. (1985). *Innovation and entrepreneurship.* London: Heinemann.

Drucker, P. F. (1988, September-October). Management and the world's work. *Harvard Business Review.*

Drucker, P. F. (1993). *Post capitalist society.* New York: Harper Business.

Gagne, R. M. (1962). *Psychological principles in system development.* New York: Holt, Rinehart & Winston.

*Gagne, R. M. (1985). *The conditions of learning* (4th ed.). New York: Holt, Rinehart & Winston.

*Gagne, R. M., & Briggs, L. J. (1979). *Principles of instructional design* (2nd ed.). New York: Holt, Rinehart & Winston.

*Gagne, R. M., Briggs, L. J., & Wager, W. W. (1988). *Principles of instructional design* (3rd ed.). New York: Holt, Rinehart & Winston.

*Gagne, R., & Driscoll, M. P. (1988). *Essentials of learning for instruction* (2nd ed.). Englewood Cliffs, NJ: Prentice-Hall.

Galagan, P. A. (1991). How Wallace changed its mind. *Training & Development, 45*(6).

*Gilbert, T. F. (1971). Mathetics: The technology of education. In M. D. Merrill (Ed.), *Instructional design: Readings.* Englewood Cliffs, NJ: Prentice-Hall.

*Gilbert, T. F. (1978). *Human competence: Engineering worthy performance.* New York: McGraw-Hill.

*Gilbert, T. F., & Gilbert, M. B. (1989, January). Performance engineering: Making human productivity a science. *Performance & Instruction.*

*Glaser, R. (1966, Winter). Psychological bases for instructional design. *AV Communication Review.*

Hammer, M. & Champy, J. C. (1993). *Reengineering the corporation.* New York: Harper Business.

*Harless, J. H. (1975). *An ounce of analysis is worth a pound of cure.* Newnan, GA: Harless Performance Guild.

*Harless, J. H. (1986). Guiding performance with job aids. In M. Smith (Ed.), *Introduction to performance technology* (Part 1). Washington, DC: National Society for Performance and Instruction.

*Jackson, S. (1986). Task analysis. In M. Smith (Ed.), *Introduction to performance technology* (Part 1). Washington, DC: National Society for Performance and Instruction.

Kanter, R. M. (1989). *When giants learn to dance: Mastering the challenges of strategy, management, and careers in the 1990's.* New York: Simon & Schuster.

Kaufman, R. (1968). A system approach to education: Derivation and definition. *AV Communication Review, 16*, 415-425.

Kaufman, R. A. (1972). *Educational system planning.* Englewood Cliffs, NJ: Prentice-Hall. (Also published as *Planificacion de systemas educativos* [Educational system planning]. Mexico City: Editorial Trillas, S.A., 1973)

Kaufman, R. (1986). Obtaining functional results: Relating needs assessment, needs analysis, and objectives. *Educational Technology, 26*(1), 24-27.

Kaufman, R. (1987, October). A needs assessment primer. *Training and Development Journal.*

Kaufman, R. (1988a, July). Needs assessment: A menu. *Performance & Instruction Journal.*

Kaufman, R. (1988b). *Planning educational systems: A results-based approach.* Lancaster, PA: Technomic.

*Kaufman, R. (1988c, September). Preparing useful performance indicators. *Training & Development Journal.*

Kaufman, R. (1988d, February). Warning: Proactive planning may be hazardous to your being-loved health. *Educational Technology.*

Kaufman, R. (1989, February). Warning: Being a proactive planner could be hazardous to your "being-loved" health. *Performance & Instruction Journal.*

Kaufman, R. (1990, November). Why things might go bump in the night . . . and what to do about it. *Educational Technology.*

Kaufman, R. (1991a, May-June). The mainstream. *Performance & Instruction Journal.*

Kaufman, R. (1991b, April). Restructuring: A case that could have happened. *Educational Leadership.*

Kaufman, R. (1992a, July). The magnifying glass mentality. *Training & Development.*

Kaufman, R. (1992b). *Strategic Planning Plus: An organizational guide.* Newbury Park, CA: Sage.

Kaufman, R. (1994, April). A synergistic focus for educational quality management, needs assessment, and strategic planning. *International Journal of Educational Reform.*

Kaufman, R., & English, F. W. (1979). *Needs assessment: Concept and application.* Englewood Cliffs, NJ: Educational Technology.

Kaufman, R. & Grisé, P. (in press). *How to audit your strategic plan: Making a good thing better.* Thousand Oaks, CA: Corwin Press.

Kaufman, R., & Herman, J. (1991a, April). Strategic planning for a better world. *Educational Leadership.*

Kaufman, R., & Herman, J. (1991b). *Strategic planning in education: Rethinking, restructuring, revitalizing.* Lancaster, PA: Technomic.

Kaufman, R., Herman, J., & Watters, K. (in press). *Educational planning.* Lancaster, PA: Technomic.

*Kaufman, R., & Thiagarajan, S. (1987). Identifying and specifying requirements for instruction. In R. M. Gagne (Ed.), *Instructional technology: Foundations.* Hillsdale, NJ: Lawrence Erlbaum.

Kaufman, R, & Zahn, D. (1993). *Quality Management Plus*. Newbury Park, CA: Corwin.

*Keller, J. M. (1983). Motivational design of instruction. In C. M. Reigeluth (Ed.), *Instructional-design theories and models: An overview of their current status*. Hillsdale, NJ: Lawrence Erlbaum.

Kirst, M. W., & Meister, G. R. (1985). Turbulence in American secondary schools: What reforms last? *Curriculum Inquiry, 15*(2).

Knoff, H. M., & Batsche, G. M. (1991). Integrating school and educational psychology to meet the educational and mental health needs of all children. *Educational Psychologist, 26*(2).

Kuhn, T. (1962). *The structure of scientific revolution*. Chicago: University of Chicago Press.

Levin, H. M. (1983). *Cost effectiveness: A primer* (New perspectives in evaluation). Beverly Hills, CA: Sage.

*Mager, R. F. (1975). *Preparing instructional objectives* (2nd ed.). Belmont, CA: Pitman Learning.

*Mager, R. F. (1988). *Making instruction work: Or skillbloomers*. Belmont, CA: David S. Lake.

*Mager, R. F., & Beach, K. M., Jr. (1967). *Developing vocational instruction*. Palo Alto, CA: Fearon.

*Mager, R. F., & Pipe, P. (1983). *CRI: Criterion referenced instruction* (2nd ed.). Carefree, AZ: Mager Associates.

*Mager, R. F., & Pipe, P. (1984). *Analyzing performance problems* (2nd ed.). Belmont, CA: Pitman Learning.

Mazzoni, T. L. (1991). Analyzing state school policymaking: An arena model. *Educational Evaluation and Policy Analysis, 13*(2).

*Merrill, P. F. (1987). Job and task analysis. In R. M. Gagne (Ed.), *Instructional technology: Foundations*. Hillsdale, NJ: Lawrence Erlbaum.

*Morgan, R. M., & Chadwick, C. B. (1971). *Systems analysis for educational change: The Republic of Korea*. Tallahassee: Florida State University, Department of Educational Research.

Naisbitt, J., & Aburdene, P. (1990). *Megatrends 2000: Ten new directions for the 1990's*. New York: William Morrow.

Newmann, F. M. (1991). Linking restructuring to authentic student achievement. *Phi Delta Kappan, 72*(6), 458-463.

Perelman, L. J. (1989, November 28). *Closing education's technology gap* (Hudson Institute Briefing Paper No. 111). Indianapolis, IN: Hudson Institute.

Perelman, L. J. (1990, May). *The "acanemia" deception* (Hudson Institute Briefing Paper No. 120). Indianapolis, IN: Hudson Institute.

Peters, T. (1987). *Thriving on chaos: Handbook for a management revolution*. New York: Knopf.

Pfeiffer, J. W., Goodstein, L. D., & Nolan, T. M. (1989). *Shaping strategic planning: Frogs, bees, and turkey tails*. Glenview, IL: Scott, Foresman.

Pipho, C. (1991, February). Business leaders focus on reform. *Phi Delta Kappan,* pp. 422-423.

Popham, W. J. (1966). *Educational objectives.* Los Angeles: Vimcet Associates.

Rasell, E., & Mishel, L. (1990, January). *Shortchanging education.* Washington, DC: Economic Policy Institute.

*Reigeluth, C. (Ed.). (1983). *Instructional design theories and models: An overview of their current status.* Hillsdale, NJ: Lawrence Erlbaum.

*Reiser, R. A., & Gagne, R. M. (1983). *Selecting media for instruction.* Englewood Cliffs, NJ: Educational Technology.

Roberts, W. (1987). *Leadership secrets of Attila the Hun.* New York: Warner.

*Rosenberg, M. J. (1990, February). Performance technology: Working the system. *Training.*

Rummler, G. A., & Brache, A. P. (1990). *Improving performance: How to manage the white space on the organization chart.* San Francisco: Jossey-Bass.

Schaaf, M. (1986, October 24). Wants: Whether we need them or not. *Los Angeles Times,* Pt. V, p. 3.

Senge, P. M. (1990). *The fifth discipline: The art & practice of the learning organization.* New York: Doubleday-Currency.

Stevens, S. S. (1951). Mathematics, measurement, and psychophysics. In S. S. Stevens, *Handbook of experimental psychology.* New York: John Wiley.

Stufflebeam, D. L., Foley, W. J., Gephart, W. R., Hammon, R. L., Merriman, H. O., & Provus, M. M. (1971). *Educational evaluation and decision making.* Itasca, IL: Peacock.

Toffler, A. (1990). *Powershift: Knowledge, wealth, and violence at the edge of the 21st century.* New York: Bantam.

*Tosti, D. T. (1986). Feedback systems. In M. Smith (Ed.), *Introduction to performance technology* (Part 1). Washington, DC: National Society for Performance and Instruction.

Windham, D. M. (1988). *Indicators of educational effectiveness and efficiency.* Tallahassee: Florida State University, Learning Systems Institute, IESS Educational Efficiency Clearinghouse (for the U.S. Agency for International Development, Bureau of Science and Technology, Office of Education).

Witkin, B. R. (1984). *Assessing needs in educational and social programs.* San Francisco: Jossey-Bass.

*Witkin, B. R. (1991). Setting priorities: Needs assessment in time of change. In R. V. Carlson & G. Awkerman (Eds.), *Educational planning: Concepts, strategies, and practices.* New York: Longman.

Troubleshooting Guide